My Place

MY PLACE

Adventures of a Lifetime in the Outdoors

M.R. James

Best Wishes,

M. R. James '93

STACKPOLE
BOOKS

Published by
STACKPOLE BOOKS
Cameron and Kelker Streets
P.O. Box 1831
Harrisburg, PA 17105

Printed in the United States of America

10 9 8 7 6 5 4 3 2 1

Cover design by Mark B. Olszewski
Cover illustration and interior illustrations by Chuck Denault

First Edition

Library of Congress Cataloging-in-Publication Data

James, M.R. (Marion Ray), 1940–
    My place / M.R. James. — 1st ed.
       p.   cm.
    ISBN 0-8117-1097-1
    1. Hunting. 2. Fishing. 3. James, M.R. (Marion Ray), 1940–
4. Hunters — Illinois — Biography. 5. Outdoor life. I. Title.
SK33.J26   1992
799.2977'092 — dc20   92-3961
                                                         CIP

IN MEMORY OF

my father, who first introduced me to the special wild things and places I have come to know and love in a lifetime of outdoor discoveries. And to my mother, who first showed me the fascinating worlds that are waiting within the pages of all good books. Sincere thanks are due both of them for giving and sharing these lasting gifts with their only, and most appreciative, son.

CONTENTS

Acknowledgments

NUMEROUS FAMILY MEMBERS and friends contributed to the writing of this book. In particular I wish to thank the James and Bosecker clans for living most of my adventures with me; Rudy Kight and Jack Reinhart, my closest friends, for providing memories I'll carry forever; David Petersen, a fellow writer and hunter, for giving criticism and encouragement that has helped elevate these personal reflections and earn them broad appeal among all readers who share my passion and concern. I also want to thank my wife, Janet, for putting up with me during the long years I have done "research" on this book.

FOREWORD

M.R. JAMES AND I have walked many of the same paths of life, although we've never met. Some of that ground has been literal: we've both gawked at the world's largest piranha, alive and well in a motel restaurant in Pierre, South Dakota, and marveled at pre-historic sturgeon in the Snake. Most of the common trails we've covered, however, lie on figurative ground: we share a reverence for the mountains, for good friends, for jolly camps, for childhood memories of early days afield, for first encounters with particularly fine animals and fish, and for people who have branded us with their warmth and honor and love.

Circumstances account for some of these similarities. We both grew up in the country, spent time in cities, and returned to rural life. We both have passed that age where the things that matter in life begin to stratify into clearly discernible bands, while the dis-tracting fluff washes away. So it's easier for us—easier, at least, than for someone in his early twenties, someone still rolling life across his tongue—to ask ourselves, "Name ten things that count, that matter," and come up with similar lists. This explains, in part, why we've shared this common ground, why this book, *My Place*, sounds a familiar, reassuring note for me.

The other reason is more abstract, but perhaps more universal.

We're both romantics who look for those things in life with roots that run deep, with grounding, with substance, with charm and . . . romance. We both have found that something in the outdoors. If you've got a touch of the romantic in your soul, you may have found it here, too.

If you do—and I hope you do, because as a group we romantics are losing ground to the technocrats, the mavens of quick solutions, the pragmatic consumers of life—if you do, you will find a great deal of pleasure in *My Place*. By the last page, you'll think of it as your place, as I surely did.

You'll find pleasure here not because M.R. philosophizes on abstractions, as I have done. Instead, he plays the observer—to nature, to friends, to the world around him—"fitting in because he doesn't stand out," as he puts it. He notes the simple joys of a hunting companion's telltale bird whistle, of fish and birds, deer and elk, large and small, of camp life and truck rides, of patient wives and caring men. His thoughts are our thoughts; his conclusions are our conclusions; his voice speaks as our choir. And he touches on these themes so close to us without falling on the clichés that so plague this genre.

M.R. James makes keen observations and even keener conclusions. He has the courage to discuss our mutual follies and the blight within our sport, the uncouth and irresponsible, the ill-mannered and unethical, the slugs of hunting and fishing that well may do us all in. But he does so in clean, lucid prose focused through a lifetime in the outdoors.

"What once was can never be again," he notes in a poignant essay reflecting on his life and the history of men in the outdoors. So true, but an appreciative look at both can guide our decisions and actions in days ahead, and those decisions and actions will someday be the history of our children and our children's children. Reflections are our map to the future. These reflections chart as straight and honest a course as you'll ever find.

Lionel Atwill
Dorset, Vermont

INTRODUCTION

DUCK BLINDS AND deer stands, now, are the perfect places for me to confront the periodic attacks of philosophy and melancholy I suffer along with the assorted physical aches that accompany advancing age. Time was that waiting for the whistle of wild wings or the muted crunching of cautious hooves in the forest duff was a full-time, no-nonsense avocation. Lately, however, I've noted that time often hangs like an August fog between the brief moments of action afield. And I've found at such times that unless I occupy my mind with thoughts of this whole business of life and death, past and future, I begin to take the task at hand—and myself—too seriously. God, I've come to believe, didn't intend it that way.

Perhaps I'm just a slow learner. But over time I've come to discover that it's the hunting, not merely the shooting, that really matters. Or should. So what if I'm lost in some private reflection when a trio of greenheads sideslips unseen into my bobbing decoys? So what if I'm musing over human mortality when a sleek six-pointer ghosts past, hops the horse-pasture fence, and walks unheard into the pine shadows beyond? Tomorrow's sun will still rise and set as this old world spins on toward its own destiny, taking all of us—ready or not—along for the ride.

Please don't get me wrong. I'm sure what I've uncovered is neither new nor remotely profound. And while what I'm writing here certainly is not plagiarism, it's not entirely original either. Far better wordcrafters have dealt with these selfsame thoughts and themes. But for me, and perhaps for you, this fresh sharing of experiences and ideas will prove to be worthwhile.

Notice that I call this a "sharing." Some cynic will almost certainly say something to the effect that, hellfire, this ain't sharing but only the ramblings of another aging writer whose outsized ego has convinced his brain that some people out there may actually care about his pathetic scribblings. And I'll concede that it does take a certain amount of gall to sit down and say, "Please listen to me and pay attention to what I have to say. It's been important to me and I believe that it can also help you to get a better handle on what's really happening to you and me and to those things we really care about." But it is. And it can.

For the benefit of critics, I'll even add the admission that *all* writers — even those who take an "Aw shucks," self-deprecating approach — have bigger-than-average egos. At least that's true of all those I've met over the past three decades in this business of putting words and thoughts on paper. But again, so what? Successful writing always involves sharing. And since success at writing doesn't commonly come by being overly bashful, the writer who doesn't believe in himself and his words is doomed to failure.

For the benefit of readers, I'll admit that this is a rather roundabout way of stating some of the whys and wherefores behind this book. But half a century of living has taught me that it's important to lay some proper groundwork before beginning to construct anything intended to last — buildings, books, or whatever.

It's no accident that I call this collection of words *My Place*. Granted, this may sound as if I'm going to be telling you about the old family homestead or some such ground I happen to own. Be forewarned, I do some of that. But I do a lot more than that, too. Actually, the title refers to my place as a predator and an observer in the outdoor world of wild things I've come to know and love in a lifetime spent hunting and fishing across much of this continent.

And though I suppose you could read *My Place* as simply an autobiographical collection of hunting and fishing tales, and perhaps enjoy it as such, there's more to the book for anyone willing to look. True, there are plenty of personal remembrances here, but I've mixed in enough ponderables to whet the appetite of any reader seeking insight and answers along with the action. *My Place* could in fact be called *Our Place* if you're one of those people who share my feelings about venturing afield in search of life, of death, and of ourselves. And I believe you do. Otherwise you'll soon put this book aside like a gift necktie.

Those of you who have at least a nodding acquaintance with me through my other books, my magazine articles and essays already know of my place. And even those of you who don't will soon come to recognize it because you've been there. Many times. Yet usually, sadly, not often enough.

My place is the tangy scent of campfire woodsmoke that hangs bluish white in the crisp fall air; the haunting cries of unseen geese passing overhead in the night sky; the familiar sight of dogs locked on point, trembling slightly, anticipating the covey rise; the sting of wind-driven sleet as a boat works its way shoreward through a heavy chop; the taste of cold coffee, warm beer, and unidentifiable camp vittles that somehow always seem better than any high-priced, fancy restaurant cuisine.

My place is the comfortable weight of a good shotgun or rifle riding naturally in the crook of an arm, the delicate balance of a fine rod in hand, the pleasing heft of a familiar hunting bow. It is the rolling explosions of a twelve-gauge over-and-under sending shot strings after a downwind teal buzzing the ice-rimed blocks. It is the flat crack of a scoped .22 rimfire propelling a tiny pellet of lead at a plump fox squirrel cutting high in the frost-yellowed foliage of a shagbark hickory. It is the muted *thump* of a taut bowstring launching a crested arrow toward a gray-faced buck skulking through the shadows below a favorite stand. It is the swish of delicate line gently dropping a dry fly on the surface of a sky-mirrored pool inches from the dimples created by rising trout.

My place—our place—is natural and basic, undeniably real. Once it was timeless, the site of an eternal contest matching mind against instinct—with survival itself as the prize. No more. We no longer hunt and fish from a need to live; we hunt and fish mostly to forget, to briefly escape the fact that we live in a crowded, polluted world of many problems and few solutions. And also to remember, to fondly recall a gentler time of pristine days afield when each shot and cast was true. Today, although we may step from concrete to grassy field and leafy woodland in answer to ancient stirrings within us, all too soon we must step back to a working-day world we cannot control.

Unfortunately, like me — and you — our place of refuge is changing. Age and attitudes are threatening its very existence. Some of us, sadly, will live to witness its passing. I, for one, would just as soon be walking new game coverts somewhere beyond the clouds when that day arrives. But in the meantime I will do what I can to capture — and share — the place I call mine.

Join me. Enjoy. Think. Remember. Maybe, just maybe, by recalling the past and pondering the future, together we can come up with a way to postpone the inevitable.

M.R. James
Kalispell, Montana

A River of
Your Own

I GREW UP near the Wabash River, a muddy, mostly slow-moving waterway that winds for nearly five hundred miles from west central Ohio, first looping east, then west, then northward, crossing flat Indiana farmland to the northwest before finally bending southward, gathering momentum and breadth as it becomes the boundary between Hoosierland and my native Illinois. The Wabash finally merges with the equally muddy Ohio River for the short journey to Cairo and the wide Mississippi.

Just outside of Cairo, there used to be a billboard with a painting of a giant Canada goose standing in a stubble field, its head turned on a long neck so that the white cheek patch showed. Block letters beside the goose welcomed hunters to Cairo, Illinois: "Goose Capital of the World." It was a billboard that a young hunter on his first-ever goose hunt never forgets.

Back then you could rent a pit at one of the goose clubs around Horseshoe Lake for ten dollars a day. The pits were in partially picked cornfields or fields of winter wheat, and each had several dozen goose silhouettes in front of it. Maybe a dozen or so full-body decoys, too. And there was a charcoal heater in one corner of each pit, infernal contraptions that seared one side while the other froze. But the heaters were nonetheless welcome on certain late November mornings when frost lay heavy on the fields and the ground beneath your boots was frozen rock-solid.

You would walk to the pits in darkness, clutching a worn Remington twelve-gauge, weighty 2s in your jacket pockets clicking faintly against your hips with each step. You follow your father's shadowy form, welcoming the wash of cold air on your face, relieved to be out of the clubhouse glare and its prehunt clamor. Your eyes still burn from cigarette smoke and a lack of sleep. But never mind. You're on your first goose hunt, and right now nothing else matters.

The sound of distant geese in the darkness is eerie, unforgettable. Close your eyes and imagine ten thousand and more wild voices greeting a lightening sky. Imagine this gabble growing in intensity, becoming a rising cacophony that you'll still hear ringing inside your head that night as you lie in bed exhausted yet unable to find elusive sleep. Imagine, then, a rush of thousands of beating wings, a palpable murmur that becomes an audible roaring like white water in a rocky gorge. Finally, imagine smoky swirls spiraling upward against the pale dawn sky—wild birds on the wing, fighting for altitude within the safety of the preserve boundaries—then slowly fragmenting into small wisps threading out high over the dark trees to where you wait. Imagine these things and you will have an idea of an eleven-year-old's impressions of daybreak in a Cairo goose pit.

Silhouetted against a sky of glowing pewter, passing flocks talk to our decoys, their cries like those of lost souls. Close overhead, above the rustling cornstalks, strong wings fan the clear, cold air.

Then it is shooting time. To the left, above the pit across the field from us, a flock hovers before funneling into the silhouettes. Suddenly the birds flare, fighting skyward. One, two, three, finally four geese magically fold and drop into the decoys almost before the booming thunder of the hunters' guns reaches us. The distance-muted *whump-whump-whump* of other shots mingles with the chorus of the milling flocks.

Low, just ahead, a dozen geese turn toward our set. The wavering line moves closer, talking to the silhouettes. And then they are rocking in on cupped wings. I snap the safety off and stand. Somehow the geese do not see us. The lead gander appears over the Remington's barrel. The bead finds the bird's head. The shotgun bucks against my shoulder. I do not remember the sound of the shot, but the bird folds as the others flare. I do not shoot again. My eyes follow the falling goose into the decoys, watch him hit heavily on frozen ground, and I hear flailing wings among frosty cornstalks. Beside me, Dad is finally shooting, and I know other geese are falling. Then it is over. I clamber up and out of the pit and stumble to where the goose—*my* goose—lies. I kneel there beside him, smoothing his feathers with an ungloved hand, feeling his warmth, smelling his wild bird smell. Then I feel my father's hand on my shoulder and look up to see his knowing half-smile. High overhead, wild flocks on the move ride strong wings toward the Mississippi and beyond.

Back home, near the Wabash, the fall and winter rains would nearly always swell the river and its feeder streams during duck season. The backwaters flooded bottomland timber and inched across the bordering croplands, drawing migrating wildfowl by the tens of thousands. Mallards mostly. But Canadas, too, and enough pintails, teal, and wigeons to add variety to the daily bag. Times were good.

I shot my first greenhead on my brother-in-law's farm one gray December day. Sonny, more a brother than a nephew, was with me. We simply walked in our hip boots down the muddy lane to the backwater lake. We had no decoys, not that they were needed in those days. We would walk together, sloshing among floating cornstalks and husks, to where the cold, toffee-colored water was thigh-deep near a treeline in one corner of the drowned field. By standing back-to-back we could cover the entire area and wouldn't have low-flying ducks slip up unseen. But it was the birds that skimmed the treetops that offered the most challenge, moving sixty feet a second and more as they appeared overhead. Mostly our shot patterns tore empty air behind the streaking mallards, but enough birds splashed into the flooded cornfield to keep us content. And we'd shoot until our shells ran out (normally) or we filled our limits (rarely), then slosh wet and shoulder-sore back toward the white farmhouse on the hill.

December backwater is icy cold. And when it slops over your boot tops as you chase down and finish a cripple, you feel its sudden, breath-sucking chill wetting jeans and long johns and wool socks. Yet by the time you splash, duck in hand, back to where you stood, there is a clammy but numbing warmth growing inside your hip boots. And you won't feel the chill again until later when you sit on a stump beside the muddy lane, lifting each leg in turn, and the trapped water trickles cold across your backside. Later, standing shivering on the back porch while peeling away layers of soggy clothes, you notice that your legs and feet are reddish white and numb. But the pile of corn-fed greenheads on the bench beside the back door and the scent of waiting hot chocolate in the air make it all worthwhile.

We hunted the Wabash on occasion, usually at Horseshoe Bend near Keensburg, but as we didn't have much in the way of a boat and decoys and calls, the pass shooting we got was sporadic at best. Far better to jump-shoot local mallards from farm ponds and ice-rimmed drainage ditches, biding our time while waiting for the rains—and the big flocks—to fill the bottomland fields when the croplands finally flooded. I still carry the sights and sounds of those magic days.

But today I live a long way from the Wabash with my wife, Janet. Now my river is fast flowing, green, and mostly clear. Clear except when mountain rains and snowmelt swell it with dirty runoff, and bobbing driftwood and deadfalls—sometimes newly uprooted fir and spruce trees—float by below my bluff in an angry downriver rush.

The Flathead River, only half the length of the Wabash, is formed by three fast-flowing forks above Montana's largest lake, shimmering blue-white in the summer sun. To the east, the mountains of the Mission and Swan ranges stand like broad-shouldered sentinels. To the west, the undulating Cabinet foothills roll away toward Idaho.

Flathead Lake was formed by the glacial damming of the river, which is born to the north in British Columbia. There this rising stream threads southward, merging with the Middle Fork fresh from its run northwest from the Continental Divide. And finally, below Coram, the South Fork—tamed by the Hungry Horse Dam—completes the trinity of once-wild waters that runs on south to the Clark Fork near Paradise.

There are mallards here, too. And more goldeneyes than you might think. And baldpates, teal, and rainbow-hued woodies. And of course the ugly mergansers, fish ducks that most hunters ignore. The Canadas come out of their homeland, too, wavering lines against sunset skies, faint cries drifting down through sharp, pine-scented October air.

Only the backdrop is different. You and your partner can jump- or drift-shoot puddlers from the river inlets and quiet coves. The greenheads still circle overhead, talking to your blocks as you chatter the feed call to reassure them while they decide whether to make a final pass and swing into the wind above your set, wings cupped, orange feet reaching for the water. Enough trading geese follow the Flathead south so that you always carry 2s in a breast pocket, where you can reach them with a minimum of movement as a skein threads its way closer to where you crouch in a driftwood blind among shoreside willows.

I shot my first Montana mallard on my place along the Goodrich Bayou just north of Evergreen. It was a lucky one-shot double, actually, made after belly crawling sixty or seventy yards to the water's edge from the dirt lane leading to our house on the bluff. I kept a trio of small pines between me and the feeding ducks, four rakish drakes and two drab hens. As I raised and the startled birds fought gravity, I picked one greenhead, as always, and sent a string of steel 4s his way. Yet two drakes fell. So I didn't bother with the other barrel. Two drakes were plenty for Janet and me. And I waded to fetch them while a cock pheasant crowed from the brushy tangle across the way.

Some disbelievers say there are no bayous in Montana. Others of us know better. In December, especially, and January after the season ends, the spring-fed bayou below my bluff is alive with ducks. I can stand at my front door and hear their duck talk in the near distance. And more than once Dave and I, like other generations of fathers and sons, have crouched side by side in a brushy bayou blind, eyes skyward, watching. Watching. Our blocks bobbing gently in a morning breeze that riffles the surface and gives life to cork and foam.

And invariably my mind turns to a magic morning when I stood alone on this same shoreline, watching a cold and empty sky for more than two hours, hunter-stubborn, sensing — *knowing* — that this was a good day to be there in that exact spot. Watching. Watching until a flock of mallards swept low over the trees, banked, and rocked in even as another flock wheeled past. And another. And another. Until the morning sky and the water were alive with the sounds of hundreds of feeding mallards.

And I simply stood there, awed, unmoving, transfixed. The Citori on my shoulder was forgotten. Recalling other mornings along muddy Midwest backwaters, I reveled briefly as only an old wildfowler can in the sheer beauty of it all. Then I simply turned and walked away, smiling at the roar of wings and alarmed quacking behind me as the mallards swarmed skyward. They'd be back on the water before I reached the dirt lane. And, God willing, I'd be back another late fall morning, too.

Later, reaching my door, I paused for a time to simply listen to them and the rush of cold river water passing below. All of us who love the ways of the wild, I have come to realize, should have a river of our own. No matter where it flows.

Two

Things I'll Never Understand

THE LONGER YOU live the more you come to realize that certain questions—besides those of a rhetorical nature—simply aren't meant to be answered. And I'm not just talking about the curious mysteries of nature, although I would like to hear an intelligent explanation unraveling the secrets of how migrating wildfowl can travel thousands of miles yet return wing-weary but unerringly to their exact nesting sites year after year, or how the salmon swim back from some sea's vastness to spawn and die in the very waters that first gave them life. No, I'm speaking more here about the unusual mysteries we encounter in the field and forever puzzle over afterward.

I know I'll always wonder about those eerie, moving lights of the Bonpas bottomlands, about how the panthers found their way to Illinois, and about how Sonny came to shoot himself that fall day when his shotgun seemed to act with a mind of its own. These remain my personal puzzlements.

Of all the growing-up places I walked and came to know intimately, none held more meaning, or mystery, than the twisty, tree-lined, shadowy waterway we simply called the Bonpas. You didn't pronounce it the way it looks, though. You said "Bum-paw" or the Wabash and Edwards County natives would know you were an outsider just as surely as the folks up in Lawrence County laugh at people who don't properly pronounce their own Embarras River as the "Am-braw." Don't ask me why. That's just the way it was. And probably still is.

I shot my first twelve-gauge on the banks of the Bonpas. I'd tagged along with Dad on a squirrel hunt, and after he'd collected enough bushytails for Sunday dinner, I pestered him to let me shoot the aged autoloader that had once belonged to Doc Couch and had accounted for a passel of Wabash County quail over the years. I was five or six at the time and didn't know that this particular gun was once used to teach Missouri mules to kick. But I found it out after whining enough to convince Dad that I needed a hard lesson his words alone couldn't teach. Soon I was picking myself up out of the leaves, my right shoulder numbed, ears ringing, jaw aching, tears welling, a taste of blood in my mouth.

"It's no toy," was all he said.

It was enough.

I later killed my first fox squirrel in the Bonpas bottoms. And my first greenhead there on Willie's farm. And my first cotton-mouth, too. But when I think of the Bonpas these days, I think mostly about the lights.

We'd often arrive early in the brittle cold of November black-ness, cutting the headlights and parking by the big oak along the gravel road near where a tractor trail led off into the blacker timber standing beyond the fields of picked corn. I cut pulpwood there one summer, sweating the weeks away loading old pickups and rattletrap trailers while the chain saws snarled and rattled around me. But you don't sweat in November. You sit huddled in the truck's front seat, soaking up the last of the heat while waiting for the first trace of a new day to stain the eastern sky. There will be time enough then to step down out of the cab, uncase our shot-guns, grab the decoys, and plod to the blind waiting beside a shallow backwater slough. We'll have to break ice before setting our blocks in the black water, then sit shivering while waiting for the first sounds of wildfowl above the pin oaks.

From the gravel road where we park you can see for several miles across the frozen fields to where a light winks in some distant farmyard or a natural gas flare dances brightly beside an unseen oil well, its pumping unit rising and falling, rising and falling in the cold darkness. When the stars are hidden beneath a blanket of clouds, these occasional lights are all you can see. At least that's what I had always thought.

But farm lights and flares don't run back and forth across the far horizon like some one-eyed vehicle gone berserk in the night. And the lights I first saw one morning did exactly that, coasting eerily for hundreds of yards where no roads run, jerking fitfully as if undecided on an appropriate destination, then racing back to where the first pinpoint of light had appeared. Elbowing Noel awake, I pointed out the moving lights. Together we watched them dance and wondered aloud about their source. That was only the beginning.

I watched those moving lights dozens of times over the years, alone at times but with enough others—including Noel, Rudy, and Sonny—to know it wasn't just my imagination. It wasn't swamp gas or a UFO or atmospheric mirages or anything of the sort.

They were distant, brilliant lights that moved where no light, much less movement, should have occurred. And then there was the cold, moonlit morning when the lights finally came to us.

We coast to a stop near the leafless sentinel oak, earlier than usual, and while my hunting buddies soon slump dozing in the seat beside me, I sit looking for the moving lights to appear in the far distance. They don't. And as the long minutes pass like someone pouring cold sorghum, I grow increasingly disappointed. The lights, I know, are less regular than Old Faithful, but I see them far more often than not.

Then, just beyond the weedy banks of a drainage ditch less than a quarter of a mile down the road, I see the light of what appears to be a farm tractor begin moving slowly along the narrow waterway. Curious about what the tractor is doing in a picked and frozen field at this time of morning, I crank the window handle a turn or two to listen. Nothing. The night is as charged with silence as a country graveyard. And no tractor is that quiet.

So it's not a tractor, I think, groping for a logical explanation. Okay, it's the light from some duck hunter's boat moving down the ditch.

But even as I reach for the keys still dangling from the ignition and twist the cooling Ford engine back to life, I know it isn't a boat. I know it is *the* lights. Just as I know I have to see the source for myself.

My mind is racing as I neglect the headlights and pop the clutch. Spinning rear tires raise twin rooster tails of gravel. My buddies come suddenly to life beside me, see the brilliant light glowing from the ditch just ahead, tempting us, beckoning us. And immediately they understand what I am doing.

No, this definitely is no farm tractor. And any duck hunter using the ditch to reach the Bonpas would put in at the iron bridge just ahead of where we parked, not row or pole a boat needlessly for a mile or more from the next gravel road over. No, this growing light is something else, something different, something unexplained. And as the dark Ford hurtles through the moonlight toward the looming framework of the rusty steel bridge, I grip the steering wheel with a special fascination — and dread anticipation — watching the drifting light float closer. And closer.

The light vanishes just as I brake the Ford to a sliding, gravel-grinding halt. A silvery ribbon of icy water flowing slowly below the span stretches silently away. The picked cornfield beyond the bridge, washed in silvery moonlight, is empty as far as we can see.

I never saw the lights again. But later that morning, huddled in our blind, we heard someone—or something—walking through the frozen leaves just out of sight across the brush-clogged slough. This was no four-legged animal, we would later agree; it was walking erect on two legs. And as the crunching came steadily closer, we each strained to pick up a hint of movement through the tangled clumps of leafless waterbrush. Suddenly there was a creaking of ice, a low groan, and a sharp cracking sound followed by someone, something, falling heavily through the surface ice and splashing briefly in the shallows; then we heard footfalls in the brittle leaves, receding footfalls that soon faded into a woodland nothingness.

We collected our decoys and left early that morning.

I saw the Illinois panther about four miles from that spot. It loped across a moonlit pasture in those long, unmistakably feline bounds one August morning while I waited alone in my parked Ford for light enough to enter the squirrel woods. The sight of that big cat was almost enough to make me change my mind. But I never saw him again.

I didn't mention the panther to many people outside my family. After all, I had no proof of the sighting, finding only occasional scuffs where the cat had loped, no clear pad marks—nothing but the vivid memory of the dark feline form bounding easily across that empty pasture. And panthers aren't exactly common in the Midwest. So I lived with the knowledge of what I'd seen until the night when a neighbor working a field near my in-laws' farm rounded a turn and saw not one but *two* panthers in the sweeping glare of his tractor's lights. Janet's folks, Eugene and Marjorie, said he was still pretty upset when he came banging on their door to tell what he'd seen. Others may have doubted his tale. I didn't need to be convinced.

Of all the puzzles, none is as mysterious as what really happened the afternoon my nephew Sonny and I decided to hunt bottomland rabbits along the same drainage ditch where I had last seen the lights.

I park the Ford, open the door, and begin pulling on my boots when Sonny walks around from the passenger side carrying his loaded single-shot twelve-gauge in the crook of his arm. I don't actually see it go off, but I jump at the shotgun's roar as sand kicked up by the muzzle blast stings my face and hands.

"Watch out!" I scream. It is a stupid warning. I am more afraid than angry.

But Sonny simply stands there, staring down at the dime-sized hole centered in the toe of his boot.

"I shot myself," he says matter-of-factly, leaning back against the dusty Ford, the color slowly draining from his face.

I gently lift his foot. A twist of heavy sock juts through the hole in the boot's gummed sole. And when we carefully unlace and remove the boot and ruined sock, we stare with detached fascination at the damage created by the full charge of 6s.

What is left of Sonny's middle toe—the nail and first joint— dangles by a fleshy thread. The rest has simply disappeared. Sonny's second and fourth toes are powder burned. And some flesh from the fourth toe has vanished, too, exposing the white bone beneath. What surprises us most of all is the almost complete lack of blood.

By the time I race back to the white farmhouse on the hill, Sonny sitting beside me and gently holding his toe as the Ford bounces over washboard roads, half a dozen single drops of dark, ropy blood have fallen onto the floor mat. That is all.

Telling my sister her only son has just shot himself—but he is all right, *really*—becomes a dam burst of words gushing forth as Margie brushes past me to the car where Sonny still sits delicately holding his destroyed toe. And soon the three of us are speeding toward town in a cloud of dust and gravel.

Sonny lost that toe and spent some time on crutches. The doctor said he'd picked the perfect toe to shoot off because his remaining toes would close in to fill the void and he wouldn't be left with a limp. Today, unless you take time to count instead of just glancing at his bared foot, you wouldn't notice one toe is missing. And after his hard lesson in firearms safety, you won't find a more careful, conscientious hunting partner anywhere.

But the how and why of the accident still haunts me. The shotgun's hammer hadn't been cocked. Sonny's finger wasn't even inside the trigger guard. The gun's barrel had been very close to the boot because the shot string fired through the full choke had no time to expand. Yet Sonny swears he had not carelessly rested the barrel atop his boot. The shotgun, it seems, had simply discharged—undeniably, inexplicably—changing instead of ending a life.

I don't really believe that the accident and the eerie lights of the Bonpas bottomlands are in any way connected—except by my presence at that same location. But in the shadowy corners of my memory, I can see a row of dark trees standing where ghost lights move on quiet winter nights, where large cats prowl, and where a shotgun's sudden blast reminded two teenagers of life's fragility—and mystery.

THREE

Trout Streams of the Mind

I CAN'T REALLY remember the first fish I caught, probably because I was too young to be duly impressed at the time. But there are dog-eared photos in the family album showing a very young me squinting into summer sunshine while proudly holding up a variety of freshly caught finny prizes for the Brownie. Small boys and fish go together like bare feet and mud puddles after a late spring shower.

Bluegills and redear sunfish are Everyman's fishes. For the most part, they're easy to catch, too. And though they won't be very big, rarely reaching the size of a man's palm, catch enough and you've got the makings of some mighty fine eating there on your stringer. Catfish—bullheads and flatheads and channels—are favorites, too. Crappies and walleyes are fine if you have a boat and hit them when they're of a mind to bite, but it's bass and trout and the other fancy-pants game fishes that get most grown-up folks' attention. For my money, I don't really care what I'm fishing for. The doing, the getting a line wet, matters far more than the end results.

But back in Illinois where I grew up, we fished a lot of muddy farm ponds and creeks and Wabash tributaries, more for food than for sport. And I can't remember a summer when we didn't have a big fish fry after Dad and my brothers-in-law, Raymond and Willie, and some of the neighbors pulled in one or more chicken-wire traps, baited with ears of corn, packed with perch and catfish. We kids helped with the cleaning chores in order to claim the transparent air bladders—we called them "fish floats"—so that we could play games with them in stock tanks and rain barrels. Meanwhile, Mom and my sisters, Margie and Melba, and the other women deep-fried the tender, carefully boned white meat in pans of roiling dark oil. And when it was time to eat, no one had to call us a second time. God Himself had to be a fisherman to create something that tastes as good as freshly caught, freshly cooked fish.

Nephews Sonny and Ron and I would walk down dusty tractor trails to the banks of the Bonpas and other shaded waterways, long poles over our shoulders, carrying tin cans full of black dirt and red night crawlers. We'd cut green, Y-shaped branches for pole holders, push them into the soft, warm mud, and impatiently bait out hooks, wiping dirty, worm-slick fingers on our shirts and jeans. Then we'd throw our lines into the brown water and settle back against some thick-boled oak to swat skeeters and wait. One can do a lot worse than to fish tightline for catfish while a summer afternoon winds down with the sound of quail calling in the distance and the dying sun turning the water from ink to chrome where its rays slant through a tangle of tree branches and touch the winding waterway.

I do remember my first trout. I caught it, a foot-long brown, in Florida at a fish camp on Mud River when I was maybe nine or ten. My folks and I went south every winter, leaving the day after Christmas and heading home the first or second of January. We'd crisscross the peninsular state, visiting friends near Lakeland and Daytona Beach. During one such stopover we took casting rods and went fishing. The trout hit the shiner on my hook, and I horsed him in. That's about all I remember.

We used to head for Texas on a semiregular basis, too, visiting Uncle Ray and Aunt Roberta (we called her Aunt Birdie) at Galveston. Usually we'd spend a full day riding a charter boat forty-five or fifty miles out in the green Gulf to the snapper banks. I remember these daylong excursions more vividly than those Sunshine State fishing ventures.

We'd chug out of the quiet harbor at daybreak and head toward the rising sun, hanging orange and round beyond a haze of backlit cirrocumulus clouds. We'd take turns trolling for silvery kings in the frothy wake churned by our passing while dark dolphins played follow the leader near the speeding boat's bow. Occasional shouts of "Strike!" caused the charter captain to suddenly cut the boat's power, giving some lucky troller an opportunity to bring his catch to the waiting gaff. I once caught a sleek fourteen-pounder, an appropriate trophy for a fourteen-year-old.

But it is the snappers I remember best. After the long ride across the unmarked waters, the captain would slow the boat to a stop as a mate tossed a marker buoy over the rail. "We're here," he'd announce. "Bait 'em up."

Coffee cans filled with cut squid appeared. Dutifully we pushed slimy bait wedges onto the two hooks on each line, one at the line's end and the other tied about two feet higher. The oversized saltwater reels would hum while weighted lines went down about a hundred feet to the Gulf's sandy bottom. Then we'd crank the reel handles a turn or two. And wait.

The wait was usually short-lived. Hungry red snappers soon found the squid chunks, hooked themselves, and were hauled struggling to the surface. We'd stand at the boat's railing for hours, staring down at where our lines disappeared into the transparent, green water, waiting for the tugging we knew would come, then cranking and cranking until the fish—sometimes two at a time—appeared below, growing larger with each turn of the reel handle.

We'd return before dark, sunburned and arm-weary but satisfied, our day's catch cleaned and iced in the boat's coolers. And even after we were ashore, separating gear and claiming our fish, we'd still feel the pitching of the green Gulf waters beneath our feet.

One summer morning the man on my right at the boat's railing was having one of those magical days all fishermen dream of. The snappers around his line fought to be impaled and hauled aboard two at a time while the rest of us, scant feet away, settled mostly for singles. He was smiling, sweating. And then as he reached for yet another hooked snapper, his hand hesitated, stiffened, and his entire body arched rigidly and collapsed backward in convulsions. Aunt Birdie, a nurse, knew a heart attack when she saw one. She took full charge, calmly and efficiently, ministering to the stricken man even as the captain radioed the Coast Guard and pointed the boat's bow shoreward.

The man soon recovered enough to apologize for spoiling the day for the rest of us. And before we reached port he was insisting Aunt Birdie keep his catch of snappers as his way of saying thanks. I stood back, watching the pale stranger and thinking about what had happened. Although I had no way of knowing for sure, I believed he was the kind of man who wouldn't have minded dying aboard a boat while reaching for a fish. I've since come to know a lot of people who would agree that there are far worse ways to leave this life.

While I was in college in southern Indiana, on certain spring days when the urge to be outdoors overcame the ability to stay caged in stuffy classrooms, a friend and I would cut classes, load up our twelve-foot boat, and head for the nearby strip-mine pits. We'd put in and row to where we could reach either bank with lazy casts, then sit for hours tempting largemouth bass and sunfish with dry flies and crank baits. We learned more beneath those blue skies than we ever could behind plaster walls.

A creepy cricket made from a small piece of sponge with rubber bands for legs, over a No. 6 shank hook, always was irresistible to panfish. Lay the cricket in calm water just beyond a cattail clump and—*wham!*—it would disappear in a swirl of green water. Even a pan-size bluegill feels king-size on two-pound test at the end of an eight-foot bamboo fly rod.

My best bass spin bait was a jointed silver Rapala minnow. I nearly wore it out one summer in the early sixties before retiring it, scarred and strike-battered, after netting dozens of two- and three-pound largemouths that tasted as good as they had looked tail-walking across the green water.

I had some luck with a rubber frog I ordered from one of the hook-and-bullet magazines always cluttering my room. But although I accounted for a lot of eating-size bass, I never landed a true lunker, despite hooking a few over the years. But tales of big bass, like those involving big-antlered bucks, grow proportionally with the passage of time. It's probably just as well I never netted one of those elusive twelve-pounders I have felt at the end of my rod. I know now that the trophy fish would have shrunk by at least one-half between the boat dock and the taxidermist's door. Such is the lay fisherman's fate. Only high priests of the sport—or your wife—will actually boat the burly bucketmouths we all dream of.

Janet will not be bashful telling you about the big rainbow she pulled from Colorado's Roan Creek one June afternoon, or about the smaller trout I managed to coax from the same shallow hole before conceding defeat and heading for the solitude of the bear woods, leaving her to clean her trout—and mine. To the winner go the spoils. And the gutting. And cooking. And dishwashing. All's fair in marriage and trout fishing.

Speaking of trout fishing, I believe Brautigan's view of the sport—and of America—although honest and beautiful, was flawed. Maybe he recognized that fact before he reeled in his line a final time out there in California and called it a life. Maybe, God help us part-time fishermen, that's why.

Time was I could sit back in the shade, content to read Brautigan or Ruark or Papa while waiting to hear the reel's warning clicks somewhere on the rim of my consciousness. But trout fishing has changed that just as surely as it has touched and tangibly changed every writer since Walton. For one thing, it forces a man to think. For another, it denies passivity by demanding active involvement. Serious trout fishing is not for idle minds or idle hands.

Today I mostly fish and think while wading in the Flathead below my bluff, usually alone but sometimes with my son Dave. And Dave's buddy, Ray, has been out a time or two after quitting time at the sawmill in Whitefish. I cast Wulffs hand-tied in winter with Danville threads around Mustad hooks. Dave often uses zug bugs and catches three fish to my one, but I never liked flies I couldn't see riding on the moving surface and refuse to change.

The thing I like best about fly-fishing is that, as with shooting a bow, once the mechanics are mastered it becomes mostly mental. You feel the surge of the river against your heavy waders, and above the rush of water you hear the line's widening and lengthening loops sing in the spring air overhead. But as you cast upriver into the current flowing by, your mind can be back on the banks of the Bonpas in Illinois. Or in a boat drifting a flooded strip-mine pit in Indiana. Or aboard a charter boat off the Texas coast. Or anywhere it may wander across the waterways of your youth. And recalling the past reminds you of how fast this day is fading into evening.

Soon the time will come for you to wade ashore, shuffling feet over the slippery river rocks, reluctant to leave the darkening river yet content in a comforting sense of time well spent. Tomorrow, perhaps, you will return. Tonight there is still time to give thanks for trout and the hopeful dreams they stir.

No Trespassing

THE LITTLE MAN in the faded bib overalls was angry. You could sense it in his quick, purposeful stride as he crossed the weedy field behind his farmhouse and headed our way. You could see it in his face as he approached — the look in his narrowed eyes, the clenched set of his jaw. And when he finally spoke, you could hear it sparking in his voice.

"I don't like you shooting my rabbits!" he declared, with a heavy German accent likely not one generation removed from the Old Country. Then, having spoken his mind, he stood there, short legs spread, small hands on narrow hips, glaring up at the seven heavily armed but thoroughly chagrined hunters, defiantly fixing each of us in turn with a no-nonsense stare hot enough to melt resolve, if not metal. I distinctly remember wishing that it was someone other than me holding those three dangling cottontails.

Back then the legal daily limit for Illinois rabbits was five per hunter, and I suppose the seven of us had nearly thirty cottontails among us. Right from the beginning, when we stopped at some shirttail relative's farm to ask for permission to hunt rabbits on his posted land, it had been one of those memorable fall afternoons. Not only did Chris give us permission, but he eagerly grabbed his double-barrel and joined us — adults Dad and Willie and Raymond, and impatient teenagers Ron and Sonny and me. Within minutes rabbits were bouncing everywhere, and the steady booming of our shotguns marked our passage through the overgrown woodlot, along the weed-choked drainage ditch, and down into the bottom-land brier patches along the winding Bonpas. It was later, on our way back to the farmhouse, that we crossed one fence too many and incurred the wrath of the indignant landowner who didn't like us shooting *his* rabbits.

In all honesty, I imagine several of the cottontails we carried had been shot on his property. In the heat of the afternoon's action, none of us had been paying particular attention to property lines. But we should have been. And so we stood there red-faced and red-handed while Chris apologized, explaining to his irate neighbor that certainly the majority of the rabbits came from his own farm, where most of the shooting had occurred.

The little farmer listened silently, curtly nodding or shaking his head occasionally. But in the end he doggedly repeated his initial declaration that, explanations notwithstanding, he still didn't like us shooting *his* rabbits. And when, finally appeased, he stalked back across the weedy field toward his own farmhouse, he carried with him half a dozen of *our* rabbits, gladly given along with our sincere apologies as a gesture of good faith, a peace offering begrudgingly accepted.

Today, replaying this vivid scene in my mind, I realize that it may take more than good fences to maintain harmony between neighbors. Moreover, I now fully understand that private property is, indeed, private. And personal in every legal and ethical sense of the word. Trespassing, therefore, whether by design or by accident, is a direct, disrespectful affront to the property owner whose rabbits — or whose simple right to privacy — we may thoughtlessly usurp.

Thanks to the foxes and coyotes, there are no rabbits on my place. But there are numerous No Trespassing signs tacked to gates and fences. I leave it to you to determine my motives, to understand why.

It's not that I oppose hunting, God knows, or that I selfishly hope to hoard the grouse and pheasants, the deer and ducks, the trout and turkeys. No, simply put, my place is posted mostly to gain the attention of others who, as we seven thoughtless rabbit hunters did, might momentarily forget that private land is indeed private and hunting there is a privilege granted by the owner, not a right inherent with the purchase of a hunting license.

It's not that I don't sympathize with people looking for a place to hunt; I've stood in their boots, plodding across crowded and overshot public lands, knocking hopefully on rural doors to humbly request permission to try that promising fencerow for birds or that woodlot for bucks or bushytails. I've winced at the sting of curt denial. I've basked in the glow of gracious assent. Like you, I've been there. Many times.

The point is that not many of us have game-rich lands of our own. We typically must rely on the hospitality and understanding of others. And even then we often must share these lands with the family and friends of landowners.

I recall one promising whitetail patch in northern Indiana, just below the Michigan line, where a co-worker gave me written permission to hunt. My initial excitement soon turned to disappointment when I found my host had also granted permission to more than a dozen other hopeful deer hunters. But it was his land, and only my selfishness kept me feeling sorry for myself until I discovered that midweek hunts were the answer to beating the Saturday and Sunday crowds. As I recall, I arrowed a decent buck there one misty weekday evening during the November rut. People, like deer, can adapt to almost any situation, making the most of an opportunity — if they only will.

Another Hoosier farm I hunted, all six hundred acres of it, was mine alone during the archery season. The landowner was a deer hunter himself and kept it posted, denying permission to all except kinfolk. If I hadn't been renting a small piece of his farm, he'd likely have turned me down, too. But he didn't know much about bowhunting and gave me the go-ahead, cautioning me to help him keep an eye out for trespassers. I gladly agreed, knowing full well he didn't think I could kill any of his deer with a bow and arrow. But I fooled him.

The thing I remember about that place and another large farm where I had exclusive hunting rights was that there were times when I wished I weren't alone. Hundreds of acres are a lot for one bowhunter to cover. I'd gladly have given up a portion of my solitude in return for a handful of good hunting partners, people who respect one another's stands and who go out of their way to help prove to the landowners that they were not unwise in giving permission to hunt. Even total strangers, wandering to and from their stands, can help you by keeping the deer moving. I could retire if I had a dollar for every deer shot thanks to some restless soul pushing it past a stationary, patient hunter who understands how to play the waiting game and use other hunters to his advantage.

Over the years I've come to discover that most often respect and permission go hand in hand. Although there are bound to be exceptions, I can point to dozens of cases where a hunter guarantees a future place to hunt because he treats the land like his own, treats the landowner like a friend if not family, and gives something back each time he takes something away.

Put yourself in a landowner's shoes. Picture a man or woman who works hard and has far better things to do than close gates and mend fences and pick up trash after thoughtless people. Imagine how you'd feel to discover tire tracks cutting across your crop fields, a gut pile in your orchard, an unrecovered deer sprawled stiff and dead in your woodlot. Think of how you'd like to hear birdshot rattling off your roof, find bullet holes in your mailbox, hear the sudden booming of nearby guns, see armed men marching through your backyard.

Picture all these things the next time you pull into some rural driveway to ask for permission to hunt. Think of them as you feel cautious eyes sizing you up. And remember them when you're turned down. But especially remember them when you're given permission to hunt. Permission is a beginning, not an end. And with it come certain responsibilities. Your future — perhaps the future for all of us — depends on how well you handle that responsibility.

The last buck I shot on Rick and Jill Garton's farm was a broken-racked five-pointer that materialized in the brushy tangle to the right of my stand in a leafless walnut tree one cold November morning. He moved in to nose the doe urine I'd splashed in the fresh scrape perhaps an hour before he appeared. I shot him at eighteen yards, field dressed him, and walked back uphill to where I'd parked my car in the Garton farmyard.

Rick graciously helped me load the buck, and Jill and the girls came out for a look before I headed for the check station. All hunters should have such pleasant hosts. But I always worked at making sure I'd be welcome back, season after season. Although it wasn't much, I always dropped off some choice cuts of venison, stopped by at Christmas with some little thing for the family, and kept in touch throughout the year, not just during hunting season. Simply put, I always did what I could to show the family I truly appreciated being allowed to hunt their land. Because I did. And it wasn't just that I was trying to guarantee a future place to hunt whitetails, although that certainly was part of it; I also did what I did because it is just good manners to do things for people you like.

There's nothing new or secret here. It just involves common sense and common courtesy. Call me old-fashioned, but I believe in the Golden Rule and feel its message is important for hunters to remember and practice. I also wish more people said "please" and "thank you" and really meant it. Showed it, too. This may not cause the No Hunting signs to come down, but it just might be a step in that direction. And I'm convinced that if more hunters treated the landowners the same way they like to be treated, more private lands would be open to hunting.

Proselytizing aside, like I already mentioned, my own land is posted. And if I happen across someone hunting there without permission, I'm going to firmly and promptly ask that person to leave, and chances are pretty good he'll not be welcome back. But if a neighbor calls and asks if it's okay to work his Labs in the bayou or to jump-shoot mallards along the creek in the lower pasture, chances are I'll say to go ahead. I might even ask if I can tag along. And even if I don't know the person who pulls up to my cedar house on the bluff, gets out, ignores the barking dogs, and walks up to ask permission to fish or hunt, odds are I'll say it's all right, to go ahead, to be my guest. All I ask is that the stranger treat my place the way he'd treat his own.

Again, good manners and common sense can work wonders when thoughtfully applied. Just understand one thing: If I do say no, I have my reasons. I may take the time to explain. I may not. Either way, it's my place and I have the right to do with it as I please.

True, you may drive away disappointed, believing I'm someone who wants to keep a good thing to himself. That's not it at all. My reason may be that I've already given permission to others just like you and I don't want more people than the land and game can handle. It may be that I have livestock in the lower pastures and don't want guns going off around them. It may be that the last people I allowed on my place didn't treat it very well, and I'm still upset. Disappointed. Whatever the reason or reasons, I am the one to make the final judgment. And I will.

Agree or disagree, you need to remember that I, for one, am on your side. I am a landowner who hunts, who knows that game populations are a renewable resource, who understands the value of harvesting a wildlife crop, who shares the belief that the animals on my place are not really mine but everyone's. Keep that in mind. Just don't ignore my fences and walk my land and shoot my game without my permission.

I did that once myself, until a little farmer in faded bib overalls taught me a lesson I've never forgotten.

A Letter Home

DEAR RUDY,

Thanks for stopping by the funeral home. Seeing you again after so many years unleashed a whole flood of memories about all the times we've spent together, good and bad. Then, just after I got back home and began thumbing through the old family albums, I came across a dog-eared picture of you and me standing there grinning at the camera, holding our daily limits of Bonpas bushytails — taken back in the fifties, I suppose. That photo — and the talk we had at the funeral home — made me do a lot of thinking. I just had to sit down and write about what's on my mind.

You remember how much time we spent hunting together? You and me. Noel, too. Every time August 1 rolls around I still think of the opening day of squirrel season back in southern Illinois. Just as the first of October I think of us packing our bows and camo and heading for some Pope County deer camp in your overloaded old green Chrysler.

I still have that blue umbrella tent we used. You remember it? I can't look at that old tent without recalling the night we were playing cards, sitting there around the hissing Coleman lantern, when the light started moving on its own, tipping to one side like some One Horse Gap ghost had hold of it. Remember that disbelieving, "Did-you-see-that?" look on Noel's face? I can still see him reaching for the hatchet with one hand and the light's bail with the other. Thank God he used the back of the hatchet and not the blade to pound the tent floor after setting the lantern aside. I bet that mole had a helluva headache the next day!

Anyway, after hearing you talk about your son, Brandon, I got to thinking about the time fathers and sons have together, and how short it really is. You know that Dad was always busy making a living, and I can't begrudge him that. But remembering the all-too-brief times he and I shared in duck blinds and goose pits, squirrel woods and rabbit patches, I can't help but wish there'd been more.

Dave's the only one of my kids who hunts, although I think Cheryl would have picked up on it if she hadn't been so busy with school and sports. And Dan sure does like to fish when he finds the time, although it's mostly alone or with his friends. Jeff, on the other hand, with all his allergies, never did get along well with

Mother Nature. And although I spent time with all of them, showing them how to shoot a bow and gun, bait a hook, pitch a tent,
build a fire, and do all the other things that come so easily for you
and me, the passion just wasn't there. And Lord knows you don't
want to push them — can't push them. You must simply be there if
and when they ever want you to show them something more.

Dave used to go scouting with me. And he sat on a deer stand
beside me a few times, too, even though it's hard for a youngster to
sit still for very long. It wasn't much later before he wanted his
own hunting bow — not one of the cheap kids' bows but an honest-
to-God hunting bow. So he saved his chore money, and I helped
out a little, and before long he had a Jennings compound and a
dozen Easton arrows.

The bow pulled about fifty pounds, I guess, and it was all
Dave could do to draw it two or three times during an evening's
practice session. I remember how he once started to cry with frustration, but I simply said he couldn't rush into bowhunting, that it
took time and patience and lots of practice. I said before long he'd
be able to shoot his bow as easily as I did my own. And before long
he could.

Still, I wouldn't let him take a practice shot of more than
fifteen yards. I told him that when he proved he could shoot well
enough to take game at short range, then we'd talk about his moving back. I don't think he liked it much, but he didn't argue, and he
killed a whitetail buck, a mule deer buck, and a black bear with the
first three arrows he ever shot at big game.

I was there at his side when he shot the muley and the bear,
and I was hunting close by when he arrowed the whitetail — close
enough to help him work out the blood trail and tag his first deer.
Believe me, these are things a father never forgets.

Funny, but Dave was in his late teens before he ever saw me
shoot anything with my bow — except small game and rough fish.
We were hunting a Wyoming water hole for antelope. I had a blind
at one corner of the stock pond, and Dave's blind was just across
the way. A good buck finally showed, and I got a perfect double-
lung hit at just over twenty yards. He ran up over the embankment
and went down in the sage less than fifty yards away. I was to him
almost before he fell. And Dave was right there, too, as excited for

me as I would have been for him if he'd made the shot. And the next day, when I was in Rawlins dropping off my pronghorn at a meat locker, Dave shot a buck of his own from the blind I'd used. I later wished I'd been there to share the moment, but I knew there'd be other times. And there were. If I were to die tomorrow, I know Dave would have lots of good memories of our hunts and times together. I hope you and Brandon can have some of the same kinds of special moments Dave and I shared.

What troubles me is how my other youngsters would remember me. Sure, I was there for Little League and junior high and high school sports. Like Dad, who was always so busy with his work but who always found time to be present when I played ball, I made time, too. Maybe he wouldn't make it there for the tip-off or opening pitch, but before the game was over I'd glance up in the stands and see him in the bleachers. It meant a lot to me.

I was as proud of all my kids for their accomplishments as any parent could be. I'll never forget Jeff's cross-country teams, Dan's games at point guard and quarterback, Dave's wrestling matches, Cheryl's gymnastic meets. And even though I rarely got to see any of them perform at the college level, I did see Dan hit his last home run as a collegian. That sticks in my mind along with every shot I've made—and seen made—during a lifetime of hunting. They need to know of my pride. I just wish I'd told them—shown them more—at the time.

But you get only one chance, and when it's gone it's gone forever. I only hope you never have to look back and regret anything you and Brandon did—or didn't do—during those growing-up years that slip away before you realize it.

It takes the finality of a death in the family, I guess, to make a person take stock of where he's been and where he's headed. And perhaps it's a natural selfishness to always want to have had something more out of the time spent with the person who's gone. I only know that when I think of Dad now I think of the good times together. And how he was.

Seemed he could always manage to fumble with the safety long enough to make sure I got off the first shot on a covey rise. And when a single banked into the wind and rocked into the decoys on locked wings, he'd always whisper for me to take him, leaving his own gun propped in the corner of the blind or lying across his lap. And more than once when we did shoot together, he'd claim to have missed when only a single bird fell.

I didn't catch on right away. But after a time I came to understand what he was doing—and why. Hell, I admit I've done it myself. More than once. Most fathers have. Most fathers want to.

But this sort of thing is cyclical. There comes a time when a son sees that his father has slowed with age and it's time to return past favors. That's when you start to insist he take the first shot, the best stand, the shortest and easiest way to and from camp or the truck. It's one way of saying thanks, of paying due respect.

I guess Dad was in his seventies before I really noticed he was getting old, that his swing had slowed, that his eyes and ears weren't what they had been. He was a proud man, though, and you couldn't let on you were doing him any favors. So while I wasn't obvious about it, I made sure I looked after him. Just the way he'd always looked after me.

Dad came out to my place in Montana a few months before he died, and for a week or so the old gleam was back in his eye. I saw it there when we rode around and looked at the deer and the ducks. I saw it when I saddled up Ric and he rode him up and down the two-track between the cattle guard and the stable. I saw it when he stood on the bluff and looked at the river moving past below; I saw it when he gazed at the far mountains. I saw it when I climbed into the rafters of the tack room and took down the rack of that old six-point bull I shot last year, letting him hold it and run his fingers admiringly over the thick tines and gnarled bases.

That was the last time I saw Dad alive. And now, in retrospect, I suppose he knew the end was growing near. Sure, we talked about his coming back in the spring. And after I bought Matador, the old buckskin gelding we simply call Mat, I phoned Dad and told him I had a new horse I knew he'd really like to ride, and when he came back out in the spring we'd saddle up Ric and Mat and let them pick their way down through the pines to the lower pastures where we jumped a red fox the last time we rode there near the creek. He said he could hardly wait.

I put a picture of Mat and me in his casket just before they closed the lid, and I kissed Dad goodbye. And this spring when the days start to warm up and there's a smell of new life in the morning air, I'll saddle up Ric and Mat and take an easy ride around the place, one time, just for Dad—and me. And when I'm riding, I'll remember our hunts and good times together, and I know I'll think of my own sons and my daughter, and of you and Brandon, and probably of all fathers everywhere.

Again, old friend, I thank you for coming to the funeral home—and for everything. I'll close for now with a personal and heartfelt salute to you and me:

May we live long enough to do most of the right things fathers do. And in the end may we be remembered by our children with more affection than regret. That, to my way of thinking, would make for a very satisfying—and fitting—epitaph for any father.

Six

Dogs

I CAN'T RECALL a time when there wasn't at least one dog around my place. I wouldn't have it any other way. Dogs, in the home and in the field, are fine company for boys of any age.

The first dog of my very own was a purebred Illinois beagle I named King. He was a squirming, six-week-old, potbellied prince of a pup the first time I laid eyes on him. And when I picked him up it was a teenager's love at first lick. I paid all of six dollars for him, and he rode home from Saint Francisville with me on a folded towel in a cardboard box carefully placed on the car seat beside me.

We were together only a short while, really. A town, even a small town, is no place for a hunting dog. So in time we found King room to range unchained—a canine Prometheus—on my sister's farm, not far out of Mount Carmel, hard by the tangled rabbit patches we haunted together each fall. While Margie and her family soon may have come to think of King as theirs, he was always mine. After all, as with any romance, a boy can only have one true and special first. And for me, then and forever, King was it.

Remembering King, I see a black, tan, and white bundle of tail-wagging energy with a rich baritone voice. And of all our times afield together, I best like to recall the cottontail jetting from that weedy fencerow with King in close and vocal pursuit. Pivoting from the waist, feet planted, I swing right to left and roll the streaking rabbit with a single shot from the Remington pump. King almost overruns the cartwheeling cottontail, but he somehow turns short and pulls up straddling the suddenly deceased rabbit. He looks down, then up at me, dog-grinning, tongue lolling, tail wagging. His brown eyes sparkle their approval. For a frozen moment there is nothing else of any importance on all of earth but King and his proud teenage owner, together, as we should be, doing what we loved most. Just King and me.

Nice shot, he says in my mind. *Nice chase*, I offer, returning his compliment. *We make a pretty fair team*, he adds. *A great team*, I correct.

And then the special spell is broken. The earth begins to spin again. Nose down, head sweeping, sorting scents, King casts off in search of another, more lively, rabbit. I reload and move over to hoist the limp cottontail. I slide it into the game pocket of my ratty canvas coat and stand there, completely satisfied for a time, before I finally follow my four-legged hunting partner into the briers. And beyond.

Teamwork. Dog and man. Such is the magic of hunter and hunting dog. And King was only the first in a long line of hounds and bird dogs to enter and eventually leave my life.

I still can't see a Brittany without remembering Pal or an English setter without thinking of Sun. Special dogs. Special times. Special memories all dog men know and share.

But a dog doesn't have to belong to you to etch certain special memories time may dim but never erase. Across fields of my mind Ron's pointer still ranges weedy draws in search of hidden coveys. Tom's chocolate Lab still quivers, eyeing the mallard floating belly-up in the shallows, eager yet resolved to wait for the signal that will launch him into the cold water. And John's aging black Lab, on his last hunt for ringnecks, still finds energy enough to chase down a cripple and deliver it to his master's waiting hand, then sleeps through the drive back to town, snoring gently, his gray muzzle resting in John's lap. Satisfied. Content. Friends' dogs can belong to you, too. Just like your own.

Over time I've buried my share of dogs, blinking back tears as the shovel turned dark soil along the fence line above the mouth of the wooded ravine. We once liked to walk there, feeling summer sunshine and fall winds, giving and receiving pleasure simply by being together.

Helping with the birthing is always better than doing the burying. Soothing, stroking, pulling when necessary, then watching the blind, wet-slick newborn pups squirming, bellying toward waiting teats, following their noses, already on the hunt. It is a good time. A proud time.

As with people, there are good and bad dogs. While I know patience is a must with most any pup, I have no use for dogs that run deer, kill chickens, pick fights, refuse to honor points, flush birds out of range, snap at kids, chase cars or trucks, and commit a variety of other canine sins simply because they've never been taught better. And I don't have much use for their owners, either.

Growing dogs, like growing children, want and need benevolent discipline, a firm yet gentle guiding hand. Otherwise they'll get by with whatever they're allowed, testing, pushing patience to the limit—and beyond. And then, not surprisingly, they rebel when someone finally says, "Enough!" Why is it, I wonder, that people otherwise endowed with common sense might moan about somebody else's dog but mostly fail to recognize the obvious faults in their own? It's a shame everybody doesn't own perfect dogs. Like mine. Yours, too. It's always the other guy's dog that has the problem, right?

Right. I don't know how many pairs of hunting socks Pal chewed up in his lifetime, but he sure wasn't hard-mouthed when it came to retrieving quail. And I can still see Sun give me one last over-the-shoulder, see-you-later look just before cresting the hill and loping away in search of distant coveys. But Sun's whistle-deafness came and went. And when my own voice reached a particular hard-edged pitch, miracle of miracles, his hearing was restored and he'd loop back my way, checking likely cover en route.

Sun's nose for birds more than made up for his spells of selective hearing. Seeing him grow suddenly birdy, zero in on a certain grassy clump, crouch, and lock up as rigid as a white and liver sculpture was enough to make any dog owner forget minor faults. Of course, had he belonged to someone else, I likely would not have been so tolerant. But Sun was mine. And always will be.

Upland bird dogs are special favorites of mine—and of most people's. Retrievers get a lot of attention, too. These dogs are the thoroughbreds of the hunting-dog world—sleek, handsome, and quite often full of themselves. They capture the fancy of artists and photographers and grace magazine and catalog covers like dogdom celebrities. And, as I said, they're my favorites. But it's easy to admire a beautiful dog. It's more difficult to appreciate the blue-collar breeds.

Yet there's also a special place in my heart for working hounds—rangy, slobbery dogs with large heads and doleful eyes. It's partly because of King, I know. But it's also because I grew up to the distant music of fox- and coonhounds, listening to the chase unfold in the dark hardwoods as I sat through starlit nights with mostly quiet men around riverbottom fires.

Mostly the chase is the thing, simply listening to the clear belling of running dogs—which is not unlike the distant sound of wild geese on the wing, yet at the same time different. To prey, no doubt, and certainly to an unappreciative listener, the sounds of trailing hounds are eerie, chillingly feral, undeniably primitive. In truth, these sounds are a remote link with the wolflike *Tomarctus* of fifteen million years ago, the modern dog's most ancient ancestor. But to a hound owner the clear belling is both satisfying and soothing, marking a special relationship between man and beast. You know your hounds' voices as well as you know the voices of family and friends. And there's a certain pride of ownership when it's your dog that finally unravels the trail where a wily coon or hunt-wise fox took to a deadfall or icy creek to confuse its pursuers, then leads the pack on a fresh track.

Shooting a treed coon frozen in the beam of a six-cell takes little talent. A single shot from a .22 long rifle usually does the trick. You simply aim for the glowing eyes high in the naked branches, because a head shot won't hurt the pelt. And you never, ever, use a hollow point if you plan to sell the hide. After the killing shot's been made, you let the hounds nose the carcass before casting them out in search of another steaming track so the chase can begin anew.

Some people can't stomach shooting an animal put into a tree or brought to bay by dogs. They call it unsporting and cowardly. Although I think they're confused about what's sport and what's shooting, I can understand their concern. But I'm also eternally puzzled by some moral criticisms regarding what's fair and what's not when dogs are involved.

Why is it that dogs are encouraged for scenting, trailing, pointing out, and ultimately retrieving a ringneck rooster or a ruffed grouse, yet swap feathers for fur, and dogs and their owners somehow are taking unfair advantage of the game? The answer, I suspect, has to do with the belief that game birds have a chance — what some call a sporting chance — to get away, while a coon or cat or bear does not. And then there's the fact that birds are shot mostly for meat and animals for their hides. Seems to me to be another of those emotion-versus-logic arguments that are for the most part impossible to win.

Were I a better writer or debater, I could argue and perhaps convince critics that I've yet to see a flushed bird outfly a shot string. And though I can't speak for every wing shooter, I'm generally surprised when I don't walk past a dog on point to drop a double out of every covey rise. Single targets usually are easier still, even when they hook unexpectedly to the left or play hide-and-seek in fencerow saplings. As some self-confident shooter said, that's not bragging—just a fact. And to my way of thinking it was the bird dogs that did the hard part.

At the same time, I've been in on too many hound chases to believe for a moment that using dogs on game animals is a sure thing. Watching bird dogs work a patch of likely cover is no different to me than listening to a pack of hounds on trail. And though following a brace of bird dogs on an afternoon afield can be tiring, chasing a dog pack can be the most physically demanding hunting there is. Bar none. I've been there. I know.

But, sadly, I also know that it's the simple act of shooting a bayed or treed animal that upsets most vocal critics. Forget the fact that most hound chases end up empty. Forget the fact that it's the chase itself, not the killing shot, that matters most to the majority of hound hunters. Forget the fact that some bayed animals routinely jump tree and escape before the hunters' arrival. Forget the fact that coon and bear aren't bad eating at all—and that Bridger and a lot of other woodsmen favored cougar over deer or elk, or even beef. There's still the fact that some cornered animals are shot matter-of-factly without a second thought by some who, like less-than-objective observers, fail to recognize that there is—or should be—a difference between the excitement of the chase and the calculated business of killing. But the heart is stronger than the head in almost every blood sport argument I've heard. That, too, is fact.

How can you explain these things to someone who has never owned a hunting dog or hound? How can he or she possibly understand the bond between dog and human, their relationship, their love of the shared pursuit of feathered and furred game? I only know that I feel sorry for people without dog hair on their sofas or car seats.

I probably will always own one or more dogs. Today it's Frosty and Bear. Someday, when they've gone the way of King, Pal, Sun, Schatz, Misty, and all the other dogs I've owned over the years, I'll briefly say, "Never again . . . I've buried enough friends."

But then, predictably, one day I'll notice that the house or yard is truly empty. And when I hear grouse drumming in the pines or pheasants calling in the grassy pastures below the bluff, I'll think of all I am missing when I walk bittersweet October woods and fields. Alone.

At such times my thoughts will turn to litters of ungainly, romping, ear-chewing, tail-chasing pups waiting for me somewhere nearby. And from that lively group, I know, there will be one special puppy. He will tilt his tiny head, peer up at me, and lick my fingers with his pink, warm tongue as I tickle him under the chin. And it will begin all over again.

Cats and Birds

I'VE NEVER CARED much for cats. I tolerate them, and they me, but we have never been close and never will be. And even though I have owned and still own cats—as much as it is possible to own such creatures—I do not really like them. I do not like indiscriminate killers of any kind.

Last spring two optimistic but impractical robins set about the seasonal business of constructing a twig-and-mud nest in the birch tree outside my home-office window. Distracted by the constant flitting of their comings and goings, I often took time from my writing to watch the busy, patient red-breasted thrushes. Although I admired their determination, I sensed from the outset that theirs was an exercise in futility. Fledglings are no-contest appetizers to prowling cats.

Oz and Mel didn't discover the nest for several weeks until the baby robins began to create a fuss each time a parent returned with a worm or grub offering. And one day I saw both cats sitting in Janet's flower bed below the birch, staring upward, long tails twitching. It was not difficult to read their minds.

Mel, short for Mellencamp, was an unnamed charcoal kitten when Cheryl announced her intention to save him from an animal shelter fate, caught me in a weak moment (as only daughters sometimes do), and brought him home with reluctant parental approval to live a pampered existence. Cheryl named her cat for some long-haired rock idol from Indiana, and this Mellencamp grew into a hulking, loutish brute that spends most of his time either harmlessly asleep or annoyingly seeking attention and affection, ever eddying around someone's legs in dark swirls and guttural groans. Even Cheryl concedes that Mel is not the most intelligent feline on earth. If it weren't for Oz, he likely wouldn't get into trouble.

Oz originally was a neighbor's kitten, part of a litter of semi-wild barn cats that mostly met their fates under the rushing wheels of speeding cars and trucks or simply disappeared as cats sometimes do. No one mourned or cared much. Especially me. But I'm to blame for Oz's becoming a part of the family. When he started hanging around the back porch, meowing pitifully, half starved and disheveled, I simply ignored him. So he stayed, nourished by handouts from Janet and the kids, I suspect. Like Mel, Oz grew into an outsized, overweight cat, light gray with dark tiger stripes.

But his feral past was never forgotten. He remained an efficient, emotionless killer.

I know there are those who claim that a lot of modern men, especially those of us who hunt, intensely dislike cats because we view them as competitors and often regard cats with jealousy, even envy. Could be. I only know, as I said at the outset, that I cannot abide civilized killers—man or domestic animal—who have no conscience. And when I saw Oz and Mel sitting in the flower bed watching the baby robins, I knew what they had in mind.

The blue eggs had produced three nestlings, naked, ugly, gape-mouthed, and always hungry. But I knew that, given a chance, they would grow into the familiar long-legged, large-eyed songbirds that hop about our yards. So I banished Oz and Mel to the confines of the garage, where they paced and loudly protested their mistreatment. Within a week the baby robins were gone; the rest was up to them.

Back in Indiana I once saw a robin killed by a red-tailed hawk. The songbird was pecking for worms in my backyard when the hawk swept silently out of Omerod's woods, blindsided the red-breast in a puff of dark feathers, and carried it, shrieking, back to the big sycamore for a leisurely meal. Had I not witnessed the attack but simply found the feathers, I likely would have blamed the cats. Although I have no quarrel with a hungry hawk claiming a meal, I cannot abide a creature with a full stomach killing without cause.

This is one reason I no longer hunt mourning doves. In Illinois, where I grew up, I claimed my share of these aerial speedsters over the years. And like most wing shooters who have tested their skills shooting into passing flocks of darting, dipping doves, I found the challenge supreme, the results humbling. My best day ever in the dove fields—a limit of ten birds with twenty shots—speaks both of my modest ability and the difficulty of the sport. But I have no particular fondness for the dark meat of dove breast. And although I never allowed birds I shot to go to waste, I grew increasingly uncomfortable shooting these migratory rockets simply for sport. So I quit. It was strictly a personal choice. It is one I have never regretted.

At times cats kill solely for sport, too. I've often watched Oz pad by, a luckless chipmunk clutched in his mouth. I've seen Oz play endlessly with his terrified catch, at times sharing it with lazy Mel, who mostly lacks the ambition to take his own prey. They allow the prey brief dashes toward freedom, ending each with paws that pin or jaws that snatch just inches short of escape. And finally, when tired of the game, they end it with a single bite and simply walk away. At such times I hate them for what they are.

I usually resist the urge to interfere, although I have and still do. At times I step in and save some wild creature's life — or, as in the case of the baby robins, make sure they have a chance at life. This, I feel, is the least I can do.

There are those who may claim it is paradoxical that I save a life on the one hand yet take it on the other. I do not see it that way. There is considerable difference, at least to me, in shooing Oz away from the front steps where a stunned chickadee sits senseless after smacking the window and leaving an oily smear on the clear glass, and in dropping a rocketing grouse with the modified barrel just as it hooks to the left between two fir trees in the woods below the bluff.

If I could be granted a solitary wish concerning cats, it would be that their owners could trade places with some bird or tiny beast just long enough to know the visceral terror felt in the first sharp touch of needle claws and teeth, the piercing gaze of those emotionless yellow-green eyes. Perhaps one such experience would keep "harmless" housecats indoors, or belled when allowed outside, and thereby prevent the daily slaughter of thousands of finely furred and feathered creatures.

I once read that cats annually account for an unbelievable number of birds and animals. I believe it. And although I have no proof, I would wager that many of the most vocal antihunters are cat lovers with felines of their own. I would also bet that these cats are allowed outside at times, where they kill, maim, and terrorize small denizens of backyard and hedgerow without a second thought from their owners.

There is no open season on songbirds, yet cats routinely catch and kill them. There is no daily bag or possession limit for cats to observe, either. And there's no hunting license required — merely the thoughtless opening of a door. So why is it, I wonder, that cats largely escape the criticism and disdain that today's sportsmen encounter?

"Cats don't know any better," some indignant cat owner is certain to point out. "Besides, they're only doing what comes naturally."

Killing comes "naturally" for two-legged hunters, too. And it is exactly because we can discern differences between right and wrong that I contend the occasional killing we do, restricted by game laws and governed by conscience, is less damaging to our environment than the slaughter imposed by cats and their mindless masters.

Warped logic? Of course it is. But how different is my emotional contention than that of the self-righteous cat owner and animal lover who casts a blanket condemnation over all hunting? Perspective, it seems, is the key. And most keys, I've found, turn two directions with the only difference being whether you wish to open or lock a door.

The birds around my place are special to me. And I'm not talking about my hopes for taking a ruff or ringneck or evening duck on some wandering walk. What I mean is the pure pleasure in watching the bluebirds in my lower pasture and the swallows flitting in the morning air above a riverside bluff. What I mean is hearing the clear call of a meadowlark and the raspy croaking of a raven. What I mean is seeing fragile hummingbirds dance and dip around the feeder outside the kitchen window. These are the special sights and sounds birds bring me — and everyone with heeding eyes and ears.

I miss the cardinals of Illinois and Indiana. I miss their piping, one-note calls and flash of crimson amid spring greenery. But the sudden sight of a bald eagle winging its way upriver or riding the updrafts above the bluff makes up for this singular absence. And I only pray I never become complacent, ignoring the big birds passing overhead on powerful and silent wings.

Before I got here, Dave told me he'd never seen a blue jay around my place, but I've since seen several of the handsome, cocky birds at our backyard feeder. The bigger Steller's jays are more common and perhaps prettier, especially when the sunshine slanting through the firs turns dusky blue plumage to radiant cyan. But the occasional glimpse of a blue jay, so familiar a sight back where I grew up, is friendly and reassuring. They always make me think of home.

Dad always fed the birds around his place, too. He'd step outside the back door of his big brick house on Cherry Street and bang on a tin pie plate, calling his feathered guests to a daily dinner of birdseed. One cardinal would impatiently flit from the trellis to the carport roof to the feeder as Dad shuffled out, scolding Dad for his tardiness. The redbird wouldn't quite take food from Dad's outstretched hand, but he likely was as tame as any wild cardinal gets. Often, he'd remind Dad that it was feeding time. More than once Dad and Mom delayed the start of some errand or routine yard work to take time to feed their birds, especially Dad's cardinal.

Dad also disliked cats. He kept a stout throwing stick and a loaded air rifle propped near the door to deter all prowling back-yard predators, although cats slinking around the bird feeders most commonly bore the brunt of his indignation and protective wrath. Admittedly, I quite likely inherited his attitudes—if not some innate sense of moral outrage—toward free-roaming house pets killing more out of instinct than need.

After Dad's funeral was over and I had a chance to change from fine wools to comfortable flannel and denim, I shrugged into my coat, picked up a battered tin pie plate, and stepped out into the February afternoon. A bitter wind whipped the yard, sending brittle leaves scudding in a game of somersault tag. I banged tentatively on the pie plate as I walked out to empty the coffee can I'd filled with seed. The cardinal was there waiting, flitting impatiently overhead in the naked branches of the black cherry tree, chiding me for my lateness, reminding me of an ongoing responsibility.

Later, flying back to Montana, I thought of Mom's vow to keep the birds fed as Dad and I had always done. And I thought of the cloth cardinal decoration we'd placed among the flowers at Dad's grave as both a tribute and a promise.

Those Wonderful Whitetails

THE DYING NOVEMBER sun is staining the horizon and casting dark shadows among the bottomland firs. It has been a sharp fall day with a brisk wind rising out of the northwest. The wind will die with the sun and the night will be calm, bringing yet another frost, but it is that time of year. For deer hunters, it is the only time of year that really matters.

Somewhere in the near distance a pheasant crows. The white-tail buck pauses and swings his sensitive ears toward the raucous sound, listening. He lifts his moist, dark muzzle, licks it, and drinks in the scents riding the wind. Satisfied, he limps ahead, favoring his left foreleg. The buck's heavy antlers, wide and yellowish white with five evenly matched points per side, bob gently with each step.

He has spent the day in a willow thicket, rising only occasionally to relieve and reposition himself, resting from a long night spent in the company of a receptive doe in full estrus. His lust temporarily sated, the swollen leg wound bothering him again, he left the doe with dawn's first pink rays. But now, rested and restless again, he is once more on the move.

Keeping to thick cover along the creek, he limps along an indistinct trail where other deer have passed earlier in the evening. But when he reaches the spot where they jumped the barbed wire fence girding a lowland pasture, he turns and follows the fence line toward the tall pine where I sit waiting.

I am as yet unaware of the approaching buck, but later — in my mind's eye — I will reconstruct his movements, his actions. I watched the does and their yearlings pass by almost an hour ago, smiling at their gamboling antics, then admiring their ability to pick up traces of my scent as they passed downwind of my stand. The lead doe stamped nervously, pacing stiff-legged back and forth, tail flared. The other whitetails mostly watched, lifting their nostrils suspiciously, honoring the actions of the old matriarch even though it was obvious none could sort out any clue of imminent danger. A dusting of baking soda camouflages human odor better than anything. Even so, the lead doe scented or sensed me nearby and for a time paced nervously beyond the fence. Finally the small group moved off. None of them looked up into the white pine where I sat watching, waiting for a buck to pass below.

By now the five-by-five whitetail is moving slowly along the brushy fence line, past the sentinel cottonwood at the edge of my lower pasture, and into the stand of shadowy firs stretching below the bluff. His sleek, powerful shoulders quietly brush overhanging limbs. Three polished hooves silently scuff the pine needle carpet; he carries his injured foreleg gingerly, putting no weight on its ruined hoof, which was shattered by a hunter's bullet a week or more ago as the buck bounded away from the orange-vested shape. The hunter's form, viewed in grayish tones through the deer's eyes, had been mistaken for part of a deadfall until a sudden flicker of movement betrayed the man's presence and sent a danger signal to the buck's brain.

Injured but alive, the buck had become nocturnal for a time. But with his swelling neck came stirrings he could not ignore. The scent of does in season soon drove him from cover. Lust clouded his judgment. And soon he was limping after demure does, spreading his seed as he has done since his second fall. Now in his fifth year, he is a prime representative of his kind.

My first inkling of his presence is when I sense, rather than truly see, movement in the shadows to my left. Turning only my eyes, I see nothing until the stationary buck finally moves his head. He is standing seventy-five yards away along the fence line that passes beneath my tree—too far for a shot. But he is there, close enough that my heart begins to pound and my breath grows ragged with anticipation.

The buck looks across the fence to where the does and their last year's fawns have passed. Despite his wound, he could easily leap the fence. But he doesn't. Instead, he lowers his head and uses his rack to punish a scrubby pine. Bark shreds and small limbs snap as he rakes the little tree, twisting his head, grinding his antler bases between burrs and eyeguards. Sap and bits of crushed bark cling to the rack's tiny, gnarled beauty points as he finally raises his head and limps closer.

The buck is quartering toward me, less than forty yards away now, and I notice the dying wind is beginning to swirl fitfully. I know that if the old doe could smell me, this buck will scent me as well. My hands are trembling. I take deep breaths, fighting for control. But the tremors continue.

Abruptly the buck stops, turns, and begins to limp away. He does not seem alarmed, and I fumble beneath my jacket for the call hanging around my neck. I raise it and give a single soft grunt. It is barely audible above the rustle of the wind. But the buck freezes and stands staring back over his shoulder. Then he turns and slowly moves my way a final time.

At less than thirty yards he circles into the wind, moving around the brushy island beneath my tree. I am suddenly unaccountably calm. I shoot him cleanly through both lungs. He spins, bounds toward the fence, and clears it easily with a single thrust of powerful hindquarters. But he stumbles as he lands on the opposite side. He leaps only twice more, staggers, and collapses into a small, ice-crusted cattail pool, shattering the glazed surface and the late evening calm with his brief thrashing. Then all is still. I unbuckle my safety belt with fumbling fingers.

Moments later I am kneeling beside the quiet pool, admiring the motionless gray form half submerged among floating ice shards — the curve and sweep of heavy beams, the wet-sleek pelage, the sheer wild beauty of him, a dignity even death cannot diminish. I briefly touch the wound in his swollen left foreleg, picturing how it must have happened. I give silent thanks that my own shot had been swift and true.

It is full dark before I can pull him from the icy water and drag his weighty bulk to the field's edge well away from my stand tree — pausing, gasping half a dozen times along the way. I crouch and split his snowy belly hair with a keen blade, quickly remove his entrails, and wrestle to prop him upright against a pine to cool. I walk to the creek's edge and wash my hands and knife in moving water so cold it sucks my breath away. Finally, by flashlight beam, I somehow notch my tag despite numbed fingers and awkwardly tie it to a thick antler beam.

His lean, nourishing meat I know will feed us through the long Montana winter. His tanned hide will make soft gloves or an attractive, comfortable vest. And, yes, his antlers will be hung in a place of honor in the cedar house on the bluff less than a mile from where he fell, a small personal salute — not to my unnatural good fortune or modest hunting skills, but as appropriate homage to one of the Creator's finest efforts in all of the wild . . . the white-tailed deer.

I do not believe in reincarnation. Yet if my spirit indeed could return in another body or shape, and if I had a choice of what form my incorporeal soul could assume, I would not hesitate to place the whitetail at the top of my list.

It's true, I'll readily concede, the white-tailed deer does not have the awesome strength and raw courage of the silvertip. Nor does he possess the majesty or bearing of a bull elk. But, to me, the whitetail is no poseur, seeking to impress others; he is exceedingly impressive in his own right. He is honest beauty, grace, and animal intelligence incarnate. He is also, among all wild things today, a survivor with a future. The bold grizzly cannot live beyond the confines of the world's fast-shrinking wilderness. Neither can the regal wapiti long coexist with man. Nor can most wild others we could name. The whitetail, perhaps better than any other big game species, not only can survive man's presence and pressures, but is able to thrive.

And, yes, I make my choice knowing all whitetails are born to die a violent death. It is, perhaps, the price of knowing true freedom. It is a price I would gladly pay.

Readily available, infinitely attractive, easily recognized and widely respected by hunter and nonhunter alike—the abundant whitetails truly are everyone's deer. Their remarkable adaptability, coupled with their prolificity, has led to a resurgence of a big game species all but eliminated a century ago. In the wake of this deer's population explosion, it is said that today's biologists can identify nearly three dozen subspecies of *Odocoileus virginianus*. But to you, me, and most Americans, there is only one deer. And that deer is the epitome of wild beauty, grace, and cunning.

Whitetail.

"Deer cannot think," a hunting friend of mine is fond of saying. "They only think they can."

Instinct or intellect. Reaction or rationalization. It matters little to those of us whose deer-hunting passion is fueled by the telltale flicker of white in shadowy brush or the glint of sun on polished tines. Sought one-on-one by any fair-chase means, taken legally by bullet or broadhead, the whitetail is best summed up by two words: mystique and challenge.

Mystique? Talk to any deer hunter and you will hear tales of incredible, legendary bucks and their progeny that have outwitted generations of pursuers. And what other animal is so surrounded by such an aura of profound admiration, so endowed with extraordinary senses, so passionately pursued by so many? What other animal? None.

Challenge? Again, talk to any deer hunter and you will hear campfire stories of shots made and missed, of stands and stalks and drives — good and bad — related in voices edged with both admiration and awe. What other animal is so plentiful yet elusive, so commonplace yet exclusive, so temporarily attainable yet eternally unreachable? None but the whitetail.

I shot my first whitetail buck in Indiana in 1963. I shot my most recent buck this past November in Montana. In between, I have missed and tagged enough deer to populate a small herd. And in a sense I am no different from thousands of other deer hunters.

Yet I know I am different. Decades of experience have brought confidence — and concern. Increasingly, there are days when I feel I have killed enough deer. There are frosty mornings and brittle evenings when I draw down on a whitetail secure in the knowledge that the tightening of a single finger — or the simple relaxation of three fingers — will fill another tag, end another hunt, crown another season. And at times I do kill. Quickly. Efficiently. But just as often I do not shoot. Not wanting the hunt, the challenge, to end, there are days when I simply watch the deer walk away. And at such times — quite often — the heart-pounding nearness, the choice itself, is more than enough to give me satisfaction. Satisfaction that once only a killing shot could have given. That time, for me, has passed.

Some acquaintances likely would blame senility for causing me to pass up any killing shot, to prattle on about a trophy sighted and not tagged, to lend a can't-miss stand to a friend. These same people likely would fail to grasp why I routinely set out game feeders. Why I slow down approaching known deer crossings.

Why I brake and pause simply to watch a small herd of whitetails feeding in the lower pasture.

Someday perhaps they will understand why I believe that maturity, not senility, is the basis for such actions. I remain the whitetail's close friend and eternal enemy. And quite likely come next deer season and for as long as I am able, I will answer the restless stirrings. And with each encounter I may or may not shoot, offering no explanation for either choice. Because, in truth, there are those of us — givers and takers of life — who appreciate the importance of certain freedoms granted and denied. Who find a special satisfaction in the bobbing, tail-waving departure of deer as well as in the stained, silent, and trussed forms slowly twisting on a sagging game pole in cool shadows just beyond the cabin's door.

NINE

Those Magnificent Big-Eared Bucks

MULE DEER, OVER the years, have grown smarter. Or I've grown dumber. Or both.

Back in the mid-sixties, atop that chalky-faced escarpment overlooking Rifle and the winding waters of the murky Colorado, I met my first muley face to face. I was crouched near a drift fence at the time, clutching my Pearson Knight recurve, watching a clear August sky lighten as the morning sun struggled to free itself from a tangle of aspen branches. Moments before I spotted the young buck picking his way downhill toward me, I had been wondering exactly what I was doing here alone in the Book Cliffs. I was a long way from the midwestern whitetails I knew so well. But the sight of that approaching buck, a velvet-antlered forkhorn with an unusually high and symmetrical rack, quickly reminded me of the business at hand.

The buck stopped, turned, and stood staring uphill. Seconds later, I heard a pickup whining closer, clattering along a dirt two-track. The buck was a reddish brown statue until the truck bounced past and clank-rattled into the canyon beyond.

Then, as stillness returned to the high country, the muley turned toward me, took a couple of short bounds, and pulled up just across the three-strand barbed wire fence twenty yards away from where I knelt, bow arm extended and ready for an instant draw. A fence post prevented the shot, and although I didn't move, the young mule deer spotted me almost immediately and fixed me with that quizzical ruminant stare.

For a time we simply looked, each waiting for the other to make the initial move that would determine what happened next. Finally, more suspicious than afraid, the buck turned away and lurched into that distinctive tail-tucked, bounding mule deer gait I'd read about but never seen.

I may have been smiling as I swung and shot at the pogosticking buck. For an instant it seemed my arrow would intercept the deer, but it missed and rattled harmlessly into the sage. I can say with total honesty that I wasn't really disappointed as I watched that muley bounce away.

This hunt was the culmination of a youthful dream. I was ten or eleven, riding in a car packed with Colorado kinfolk, when an evening parade of mule deer briefly stopped traffic filtering out of

Rocky Mountain National Park. One of the deer was an aged mountain monarch with, to someone used to seeing only whitetail antlers, an elklike rack. It was a buck I'll never forget. And although it was fourteen years before I had a chance to actually hunt for a muley, I knew it would prove to have been worth the wait.

After the forkhorn disappeared, I crossed the fence and made a brief, fruitless search for my fiberglass shaft. Then I began angling downhill, following the fence line toward an aspen grove where gentle, golden sunlight slanted into the shadows. I hadn't gone far when a deer thudded away below. This buck was larger, at least a three-pointer, and I stopped to watch. Within seconds a twin appeared like a wisp of reddish brown smoke among the white-black of the aspen trunks.

The second buck was standing broadside at about forty-five yards, his head and rump hidden by brush and tree trunks. He'd likely been alerted by the ground-thumping departure of his buddy; however, he couldn't see or scent danger for himself and was simply checking things out. As he stood unmoving, I pulled an arrow from my bow quiver, nocked it, and came to full draw. I released and *knew* the shot was good even before I heard the hollow *thump* and watched the fletching disappear into the buck's ribs, tight behind his shoulder.

The deer wheeled and crashed blindly away, bulldozing through a deadfall and disappearing. I forced myself to wait fifteen minutes that seemed like hours before walking quietly to the spot where the buck had stood. Almost at once I saw a spattering of crimson droplets. Tracking was easy. Fifty yards along the trail I found my blood-streaked arrow. Twenty yards further I stopped when I saw a deer, a big doe, moving through an opening across the timbered pocket. I strained for a glimpse of my wounded buck, but she was alone. I was about to move on when I saw him stretched out beneath a slanted pine just ahead. He was quite dead. My broadhead had left an X in the reddish blue muscle of that three-by-three's heart.

In those days, Colorado deer and elk licenses cost ten dollars each. If you didn't want to hunt on your own, you could pay less than a hundred bucks for a week's worth of guide services, although most outfitters didn't know much about bowhunting or hunting muleys in the late summer bow seasons. Consequently, there wasn't much competition for mule deer bucks, and I know that many of the long-eared deer I shot back then had never seen a bowhunter. Some actually stood and watched you unsnap an arrow, nock it, draw, aim, and release. They seldom moved until the arrow hit—or missed just close enough to make them realize they should seek out more hospitable high country havens. A lot of those slow learners never got a second chance.

One thing I like about mule deer is that they're quite visible. In places you can see more deer in one day than you'll see in a whole season in whitetail country. And the early seasons don't conflict with serious whitetail hunting either. Another plus.

Mule deer are stalkable, too. Much more so than any whitetails I've known. Or at least they used to be. I've seen them change over the years. I guess it's for the better, because time was I felt we were taking advantage of them. Before bowhunting became so popular, before mule deer became pressured, they had it pretty easy after the last winter snows melted and hillsides turned springtime green. Bucks eating and getting fat, antlers sprouting anew; does birthing a new crop of fawns, browsing and nursing away the weeks and months beneath sapphire skies.

Then one August day there again is human scent on the morning breeze. A heavy-horned buck, working uphill to his daytime bed at the base of a stunted juniper, hears a stick crack nearby—or merely senses an unseen presence—and pauses to stare. In November, when the high country comes alive with orange-clad armies and the biting wind carries with it an occasional sting of snow pellets, he likely would have bolted. But this time he simply looks. And seals his fate.

There is a muffled, unidentifiable noise. Then a hissing, like the sound of a diving kestrel. And a sudden acute pang, an unaccountable twinge. Then instinct and adrenaline take over—too late—and powerful hindquarters push the old buck down and away in a panic rush of brush-breaking bounds. He falls once, regains his feet, stumbles a few yards farther, then collapses, slides against a young aspen, kicks briefly, and is still. His head is twisted, wet nose pointing uphill. One side of his velvety rack juts above his resting place like some strangely bifurcated reddish tree branch.

Perhaps this is as it should be. Better to live and die high and free, mostly away from man, amid some of God's greatest natural glories, than to be domesticated and exist behind wire waiting for the inevitable fate of all stockyard creatures. Picture this same magnificent buck polled, grain fed, injected with growth hormones, standing shoulder to shoulder, wither to wither with others of his kind, hock deep in feces while breathing feedlot stench instead of clean mountain air. Although I cannot speak for the buck, I do know which death I believe he'd choose.

Somewhere along the line, mule deer earned an undeserved reputation for being dumb, although some, in fact, are. I have seen small bucks stand staring in fascination at the two-legged apparition before them, perhaps even taking a step or two closer for a better look. But old does and big-racked bucks are anything but dumb. Mule deer, preyed on by cats and coyotes, bears and humans for centuries, have an innate wariness found in all wild things subjected to sudden death from fang and claw, bullet and broadhead. They are a quick study in survival techniques upon which their existence depends in an ambivalent, if not uncaring, natural world.

One year the mule deer stand along remote roadways, trusting, curiously watching or simply ignoring a vehicle that brakes nearby. Those more interested in meat than in hunting morality simply roll down a window, rest a rifle, squeeze a shot, and watch a buck or fat doe drop where it stood. The more ambitious may actually step out of the truck cab before making the shot—almost a must for bow-and-arrow road hunters, although lazy minds have learned that a pickup's bed serves them nicely, thank you . . . ethics and the spirit of fair chase be damned. Unwary deer die by the thousands in such an ignominious manner.

But the survivors do learn. And the following day or week or year they freeze at the sound of an approaching pickup, flee before it brakes, and disappear in long, bounding leaps as unhappy men mutter over the scarcity of game, complaining that deer huntin' 'round here sure ain't what it used to be.

Such people live and die without knowing true pursuit of the far-ranging long-eared deer, deer as much at home on treeless sage flats as among piñon and juniper sidehills; in the cool aspen groves of high, hanging basins; and even above timberline on windswept alpine tundra amid sterile piles of rotten granite and steep scree chutes where the detritus slides and shifts beneath hooves and cleated boot soles alike. Such people miss much.

Ideally, meeting a muley on his home turf entails getting off your duff and on your feet. Hunting mule deer most often means just that—hunting. Although sitting in a blind or tree stand and trail-watching near water or feed will work, mule deer are nomadic, less-than-predictable animals that require strong legs and lungs to reach.

Most of today's deer are shot, not hunted. They appear somehow magically and are shot at from ambush or spontaneously. Some are impatiently pushed to waiting guns and bows, by design or by carelessness. But too few hunters know the challenge of quietly roaming a muley's homeland, seeing before being seen, and easing into shooting position while a browsing buck nibbles at cliffrose or serviceberry or bitterbrush, his antlers dipping easily, distractingly, as you take a final silent step and steady yourself for the shot.

For my money, this should always be a close-range confrontation, twenty yards or less. Most anyone with a flat-shooting mountain rifle can find a solid rest, align the cross hairs, draw in a deep breath, and squeeze a trigger on an unsuspecting deer. Believe me, sending 150 grains of lead across a canyon is not nearly as satisfying as sending 145 grains of sharpened steel across a few feet of mountainside after spending an eternity getting close enough to see the muley breathe, *blink*; close enough to hear it tear the dainty leaves, *chew* them; close enough to finally be seen or heard as an arrow nestles into its familiar anchor; close enough to be aware on the very edge of your consciousness, even as all of your concentration is on the hollow just behind the buck's shoulder where you will your arrow to fly, that the buck knows you are there—somehow within point-blank distance. And the look in his liquid eye is one you will forever remember.

Ghost Bucks
I Have Known

I SAW THE walking spike first, but at that instant of recognition I caught other movement in the trees behind him and knew he was not alone.

It was mid–September and there were, all told, five whitetails in the bachelor bunch: the lead spike, a forkhorn, a sleek three-by-three, and two tentative four-by-fours bringing up the rear. Well, actually, only one was a four-by-four. The other trailing buck had four perfect points on his right side, but the left consisted of a broken main beam maybe six inches above the pedicel. Strips of bloody velvet dangled across his face, hanging from the broken antler stub and the undamaged beam as well. All the other bucks were polished out, their newly exposed antlers still unrubbed and a sickly white—the color of a newly mended arm or leg just after a doctor removes the cast.

They were moving right to left, maybe forty yards away, midway between the overgrown two-track and my tree. Not surprisingly, the spike and forky missed my hour-old scent trail as they passed, but the three-by-three stopped and nosed my tracks, likely wondering over the curious odors of fox pee and gummed boot soles. And, in turn, the two trailing bucks also stopped to check out the puzzling scent.

All this time I was standing motionless, watching, bow in hand, fourteen feet up on a metal stand in a skinny fir that overlooked the opening where the deer now stood. When the four-by-four finally walked over to check out the essence of doe urine I'd sprinkled on a spiny thistle stalk exactly thirty paced-off yards from my tree, I decided to take him.

Slowly, silently coming to full draw, I held for the mid-body indentation behind the buck's shoulder and released. In the instant replay of my mind's eye, I still see the blur of the arrow speeding to the deer and disappearing into his chest. I watch the whitetail whirl, bound half a dozen yards past other running deer, stop, and turn to stare back at my angled arrow buried six inches into the gravelly soil where it had suddenly sprouted like some long-stemmed fall flower.

Unaccountably, instead of staggering and going down where he stood, the four-by-four simply stamped a forefoot and snorted.

Strange actions, I knew, for a deer just shot through both lungs and, perhaps, the heart.

That I might have missed that buck never occurred to me. Admittedly, it never does before I shoot. Self-doubt is the surest way I know to miss something. And while it's true that over-confidence can be the bane of any shooter, gun or bow, uncertainty is far worse. At least in my book.

Long after the buck stalked off in that indignant, stiff-legged, tail-flared walk of a semispooked whitetail, and even after I climbed down and checked my arrow shaft, which I found to be whistle-clean from nock to where it buried its head in the wood-land soil, I puzzled over what had happened. I still refused to believe I'd missed. After all, I was riding the crest of a hot shooting streak—not unlike a hitting streak you recall from sandlot days, when you stride into the pitch and the baseball rockets away as if fired from a punt gun. And you *know*. You just *know*.

Standing in that fir, I knew I hadn't missed a shot in nearly two years, taking two buck pronghorns, two bull elk, a good bear, a so-so buck whitetail, and a dry doe. So, as I said, missing the shot didn't cross my mind. It had to be something else. And then it came to me, slowly lighting my mind the way the first rays of revealing summer sunshine spill over the peaks and wash shadows from the ridges below.

It had been a ghost buck. A spirit deer. And my arrow *had* passed through its chest, just as I'd seen. Yet because it was a woodland wraith without true substance, the honed steel arrow-head had no effect. Of course! It was not the first time I'd come face-to-face with such specters. Nor would it be the last.

One November afternoon, in an Indiana jungle of honey-suckle and briers where I knew several coveys of bobwhites hung out, I topped a small rise to see two sleek does standing in a weedy ravine just to my right. Neither saw or heard me. They were star-ing at a row of dark trees farther down the ravine. As I looked up, a ghost buck stepped from the tree line, crossed the swale, and turned its gaze on the does—or on me.

I didn't realize he was a ghost buck at the time, of course. That discovery came only after I had pulled back the magazine cutoff, locking the two light loads in my autoloader's magazine, fingered the bolt release button, and eased the operating handle back until the chambered 8 ejected into my gloved hand and the breech bolt locked open. I fumbled a rifled slug from a vest pocket loop, slipped it into the chamber—never once taking my eyes from the buck—fingered the bolt release again, and with a whisper of steel closed the breech bolt. There was no more sound than a muted metallic click.

The two does were still looking uphill at the buck as I shouldered the Browning and peered down the ribbed barrel, placing the bead on the deer's shoulder, pushed the safety button's enlarged head, drew a long breath, and squeezed the trigger.

Both does danced away in long, tail-waving leaps as the echoing thunderclap of the twelve-gauge bounced off the tree line and washed back across the weed-choked ravine. But the whitetail buck never flinched. Never moved. He simply stood there, broadside, still staring, his ghost-white antlers arcing up against the darkness of the trees behind him. I could feel his eyes on me as I groped for another slug, reloading quickly with leaden fingers, before I raised the shotgun a second time.

For a frozen moment in time there was nothing else in the world but that motionless buck and me. I was afraid to blink lest he vanish. I was afraid to shoot lest he merely continue to stand there—an apparition, a phantom deer incapable of dying, destined to forever haunt me. And then I steeled myself and shot again.

Through the recoil blur I thought I saw him drop as if pole-axed and roll kicking into the weed-choked ravine. And for a long time I simply stood there, watching below for some reassuring movement, something—*anything*—that would convince me I really had seen what I thought I had, really had shot at some flesh-and-blood buck and not at a woodland wraith, really would find him lying dead where he had dropped and rolled.

Finally, hesitantly, I reloaded and moved down to discover for myself what was real and what was not. And what I found was nothing. No cut hair, no blood, no tracks. Nothing. And much later, as I quickly left the ravine with an evening gloom closing in, I caught myself casting sidelong glances back into the tenebrous shadows trailing me from where the ghost buck and I had met.

Ghost bucks can be verbal, too. One cool October morning, above the noisy scratching of a pair of fox squirrels playing tag in a shagbark hickory near my stand, I heard a single soft sound—like some man unaccountably coining and uttering the word "urp"—in the multiflora rose tangle behind me.

I knew it was a buck. I slowly turned and peered into the dense cluster of trailing vines but, unmoving, he was invisible. It wasn't until he stepped into a grassy slash that a deer magically materialized. It *was* a buck. And a good one.

There was no way to thread an arrow through the limbs to where the buck stood, so I simply watched and waited, hoping he'd follow the trail winding below my tree. He didn't, of course. He merely walked straight ahead, so soundless I could swear he was floating over the forest floor, finally turning and stopping in the open sixty or more yards away. There he lowered his head and hooked an oak sapling, causing it to whip and jerk as he raked it with his heavy antlers.

Risking a long shot never occurred to me. Besides, I knew a ghost buck when I saw one. Within seconds the deer simply vanished. One instant he was standing there at the sapling's base, and less than an eyeblink later he was gone, the only testimony to his passing my memory—and a wet, white gash on the dark bark of a young oak.

This buck and others of his kind are likely the same unseen rub-makers that somehow slash the trees near our stands yet seldom, if ever, show themselves. How else can you logically explain the sudden appearance of such woodland signposts? Ghost bucks! It is the only answer.

Like normal deer, ghost bucks feel the stirrings of rut. And like flesh-and-blood bucks, they sometimes grow careless. This is the prime time for seeing and hearing them. Just don't expect to kill one. You can't kill a ghost. I've tried. I know.

One November morning I heard the buck coming through the woodlot, churning brittle leaves and grunting like a barnyard hog as he trailed the coy doe that had passed my stand minutes earlier. Then he appeared, nose down, passing broadside behind a cluster of screening sumac thirty yards away. I raised the Remington, swinging with the walking deer, ignoring the urge to look at his high, bone white rack, patiently waiting for him to step clear.

Holding for the shoulder to break bone and put him down in an instant, I touched off a shot. The buck whirled. I shot again just before he reached the sumac. Dead on his feet, two heavy slugs deep in his chest, he bounded gracefully on, flattening out in mid-air like a horse hurdling a steeplechase hedge. I shot a third and final time just before the woods swallowed him up. And then he was forever gone, the sounds of his ground-gaining bounds diminishing into nothingness among the shadowy hardwoods.

No hair. No blood. Nothing.

Another ghost buck. What other rational explanation is there? No one misses a living and breathing broadside buck three times at thirty to forty yards! Ever! Do they?

I, for one, know ghost bucks exist. I could go on and on, relating other stories of similar encounters. But the skeptics will never believe me, despite what evidence I offer. And the believers already have no doubts.

Just keep what I've said in mind. Remember it the next time you see a buck moving silently past your stand or suddenly hanging like ground fog where seconds before nothing stood. And if your arrow flies true or your gunshot is good—and you *know* you didn't miss—yet the buck bounds off untouched, obviously unaffected by lead or steel, perhaps then you'll come to understand, even to believe.

I pray that my own chance meetings with ghost bucks never end. How empty would be the victories of woodland encounters did man always win. There needs to be something stirring in the imaginations of us all that defies logic and natural laws, something that mystifies yet somehow satisfies. Ghost bucks serve such a purpose. There are some things we are better off not being able to explain or understand.

An Affinity for Antelope

THE FIRST RAYS of a late summer sun spilled over the earthen dam, chasing the shadows from the shallow bowl where a pool of water lay flat and silvery still in the early light. Slender wisps of vapor floated inches above the pool's surface. The prairie air was remarkably sharp and clean, bearing a faint suggestion of sage.

And as the rising sun climbed higher in an impossibly blue western sky, a small flock of sage grouse appeared. Clucking softly, the plump, gray birds walked to the edge of the water and dimpled the surface as they briefly drank. Then they melted away, moving back up the sage-covered sidehill, leaving only their trifurcate tracks in the damp earth ringing the receding pool. Small craters of dried mud created by the hooves of thirsty range stock, deer, and antelope pocked the cracked ground beside the precious water.

The pronghorn buck had bedded with the three does less than a mile from the water hole. It was the dark of the moon, and the animals had moved very little during the night, standing only occasionally to nibble at sage leaves or to stretch and relieve themselves. But with pink dawn staining the horizon, the four pronghorns were on the move, walking unhurriedly across the valley floor, browsing as they went.

The buck trailed the does. Now in his sixth year, he was a fully mature, handsome specimen. His ebony horns, tipped with ivory, were long and heavy; thick twin prongs jutted forward well above the tips of his six-inch ears. Ever watchful, he caught a flicker of movement and paused to stare as a coyote emerged from a ravine nearly a mile away. Even though the song dog posed no threat to the buck or his does, the buck watched motionless until the coyote trotted from view. He then lifted his black muzzle and tested the air. The scent of his does, still several weeks from the full heat of estrus, sparked a stirring within him. He broke into a stiff-legged run, circling the small harem effortlessly. Pausing, he pawed briefly at the sun-hardened prairie soil, squatted, and urinated. The does, unmindful of the buck's ritual antics, walked on, moving toward the water hole now just ahead.

Pausing on the sidehill above the shallow pool, the does stood staring down for any sign of danger. All across the valley other pronghorn bands were on the move. And though the morning was cool, the day would grow hot. Many of these same animals would eventually find their way to this water hole, one of only a few scattered in the long valley. The buck arrived just as the does, satisfied that no threat lurked below, moved quickly down the slope.

But the buck hung back, watchful. He was not really thirsty. Besides, he sensed a feeling of vulnerability each time he moved in to drink. This feeling usually caused him to pace nervously when he moved to water. He would approach cautiously alert, often covering the final few yards at a hurried run. Then, after lowering his head, he would sometimes jerk it erect again as if trying to catch the telltale movement of some unseen enemy. Finally he would drink, deeply but quickly, before turning away — water still dripping from his wet muzzle — to hurry from these ideal ambush spots.

Now he watched the does. They were standing at the pool's edge, their forelegs in the water. One by one the three does lowered their heads to drink, their soft slurping sounds audible in the still morning air. Abruptly the buck moved to join them.

A magpie flew past the drinking does and dipped to land in a clump of sage near the pond's dam. But the long-tailed bird suddenly flared and winged away, scolding noisily. The does jerked up, instantly alert. The buck stopped, staring after the bird. For a long moment none of the animals moved. Then a young doe lowered her head and resumed drinking. Soon the other does followed suit, and the buck moved quickly to join them, shouldering his way between two of his companions. After a final check of the surroundings, he drank.

The young doe on his right finished drinking and backed away, her hooves making sucking noises in the mud. The other two does soon followed, and the buck could hear the trio walking up the sidehill behind him. In seconds he would follow . . .

A muffled sound from the sage clump caused the buck to spin, powerful leg muscles bunching to carry him to safety. But something struck him behind the shoulder. He splashed through a corner of the pool in a shower of muddy water, pivoted, and raced in a half circle around the far side of the basin. There he stumbled and fell, regained his feet, then sprinted for the safety of a nearby arroyo. But something was wrong. He fell again, and this time he could not rise. Instead the buck slid, kicking and jerking, down the slope to the water's edge. He raised his head a final time, then allowed it to slowly sink back. One heavy horn buried itself in the well-tracked mud, and a large, round eye stared unseeing at the prairie sky overhead.

I first bowhunted pronghorns on the northwestern Nebraska prairie lands in 1971. And over the years I've hunted and shot enough of these fleet prairie dwellers to develop a special affinity for the antilocaprines wrongly but tenaciously called antelope. True, a mature bull elk is more regal in appearance. True, a mature buck deer is more stately in its demeanor. True, a lumbering bear sets pulses to pounding more quickly. But for sheer poise and grace, give me the princely pronghorn every time.

These unique, secretive animals are true survivors, possessing a delicate appearance that belies their gritty ruggedness. I admire that quality. And of late, out of growing respect, I've done more watching than killing.

Most antelope hunting today is, in fact, antelope shooting. Is it truly hunting to bounce across the prairie in a four-wheel drive until a herd is sighted, then brake, step out, aim a scoped flat-shooting rifle, and squeeze off a round (or rounds) until a reddish tan target goes down in a puff of prairie dust? Similarly, is it truly hunting to sit and wait beside a stock tank or secret seep until thirst inexorably draws game within easy bow range?

Not really, I'm now convinced. It's shooting. It's killing. Not hunting. I know because I've done it myself.

I once saw a buck pronghorn walk in to water near a creaking windmill. There he took a sharp broadhead through the chest at less than a dozen steps, whirled, ran half a hundred yards to a barren hillock, stood for a time, then lay down as the widening crimson stain spread slowly on his side. After resting for an unbelievable time beneath the merciless prairie sun, he stood again and slowly walked back to the windmill, the shallow pool pulling him like a magnet. A second arrow finally finished the job, but not before his death dash carried him one hundred or more yards beyond the water.

Call it what it is: shooting, not hunting. Recognize him for what he is: a tough little prairie survivor.

I shot at a drinking buck one August morning, holding for the shoulder as I released. But he heard the muffled thump of my bow and jerked his head around, catching the streaking arrow a glancing blow full in the face. The gaping wound opened beneath his left eye erupted blood — more than you ever could imagine — as he raced for the end of the dike. There he stood for a time, raining red droplets on hard-packed soil, before walking off unsteadily to bed in nearby sage shadows. And when I watched his head finally sag, only then did I put my binoculars aside and walk a wide, red-stained path down to where he lay slumped and still, awaiting my knife.

But this was a Lazarus buck. As my boot carelessly scraped the sun-baked soil, he suddenly stood and stared back at me. Then he turned and stumble-walked away while I reached for another arrow, beginning a deadly game of follow the leader until, with but one arrow left in my quiver, I shot him through both lungs and knelt beside him while he died, gently stroking his brittle neck hair and quietly apologizing for botching the job.

Again — shooting, not hunting. Tough, tough little survivor.

The last pronghorn I shot — perhaps the last pronghorn I'll ever shoot — was a lone dry doe I claimed for meat. She died on an empty Wyoming prairie the way all hunted pronghorns should die: quickly and for good purpose. My arrow caught her through both lungs at just over twenty yards, scarcely slowing down before snicking into the sage beyond. She spun and dashed away, covering a hundred yards before collapsing at full gallop. I didn't see her go down, but I could read what happened in the sandy soil of a coulee where she finally fell, somersaulting once and skidding to a stop facing back upslope.

I knelt beside her, too, brushing dirt from her lolling tongue and wiping blood from the weeping wound in her side at the exact line where the tan and white merge. Better this, I rationalized, than starving stacked against some drifted fence line with others of her kind as wind-whipped snow angles from an angry sky. Better this than being hamstrung and disemboweled, thrashing, eaten wide-eyed and alive by coyotes, though no hunter should begrudge another hunter's success. Certainly better this than to be caught frozen in the glare of onrushing headlights on the asphalt ribbons that now cut across prairie-land travel routes used for millennia by the hooved creatures—long before man and his machines arrived to change things forever.

Years ago, it was a pronghorn that I last arrowed but failed to recover. He took my arrow high through the chest, above the lungs yet below the spine in that small empty space devoid of vitals. He raced away and vanished like the prairie wind. I searched for him for hours that day, fruitlessly. But later he was back, browsing on a sage-dotted sidehill nearby, a small spot of dried blood on his side the only sign this was the same buck. And I saw him later in my hunt, too, oblivious to the fast-healing wound, going about his day-to-day business of surviving as he had every day of his life. I never got close enough for another shot, and I wouldn't have taken it if I had. Our paths had crossed; he had won the confrontation, earning my eternal admiration and respect.

Tough, tough little survivor.

Amen.

When not routinely arrowed point-blank from an ambush or callously shot by someone using a vehicle's hood or door as a rifle rest at such a great distance the pronghorn is sprawled kicking before even the report of the shot comes rolling over the prairie, pronghorns are a worthy challenge to anyone.

And sighted from afar, cautiously stalked, and fairly slain in the ageless one-on-one duel between predator and prey, pronghorns are even more: they are the consummate blend of sheer speed and delicate strength, unmatched eyesight, and a unique beauty as captivating as the harshly inhospitable lands they roam.

Yet for all of his innate abilities, the highly visible pronghorn is a relative pushover wherever he is pursued with the hunting tools devised by modern man. Therefore, it is up to each of us to decide how best to test our own meager skills against the reigning prince of the plains. To me, the question remains a recondite mystery whose answer mirrors the true nature, the very soul, of each of us who hunts. Or merely shoots. The choice is ours.

TWELVE

Bears

THE CHARGING BEAR reminded me of a one-animal stampede. I was on my hands and knees at the time, crawling through a game tunnel in a hellish tangle of Colorado oak brush and mountain mahogany. One second I had the path to myself, the next instant a black bear was rushing headlong at me from less than a dozen yards away.

At such moments, I'm convinced, it is not unusual for your mind to briefly refuse to register what your eyes are witnessing. There is a moment of hesitation, which for me could have proved fatal had that bear been attacking in a blind frenzy. Perhaps I felt the same chilling pause some unwary backcountry hiker experiences as a huge, hump-shouldered bruin suddenly appears on the trail just ahead. Or perhaps the mind-jarring, disbelieving hesitation of a stalking hunter on some sunlit African savanna at the instant he hears a coughing grunt and rustling grass, just before he turns to see the onrushing tawny form. I only know that at such times your reaction quite likely springs more from reflex than reason.

What might have happened to my hypothetical hiker and hunter is a matter of individual opinion or imagination. What happened to me is less debatable because I survived to relate the experience.

I was armed with only a camera dangling from a neck strap; nevertheless, in that mind-blurring instant of unexpected confrontation, I would have had no time to use any weapon for protection. Fortunately none was needed. By the time my disbelieving mind registered *bear!* I was already rolling off the game trail, clawing into the thick brush. I yielded undisputed right of way to that stampeding Uncompahgre Plateau bruin.

He passed close enough for me to trip or touch, had I chosen to try. Which I didn't. And then he vanished down the path I had just climbed, leaving a faint, musky animal scent. Or was it the odor of fear? Whatever it was, it hung in the brushy tunnel where I lay, heart pounding, staring up through a latticework of branches and leaves at an ink blue sky and cotton-puff clouds.

I later learned that the bear was not charging me, but hightailing it off a mountainside where he'd been jumped by hunters. The fact that I was in the middle of his escape route made for an interesting, mind-sticking moment; however, I was never, I came to realize, in any true danger.

This is not to say that bears aren't dangerous—or can't be. Their unpredictability and awesome power, complemented by surprising speed, make them a potential threat. But despite the fact that a couple of my friends will forever carry with them the whitish scars of bear attacks, I worry more about drunken drivers than angry bears.

I killed my first bear in '71, and I've taken quite a few since, on hunts in Maine and Minnesota, Michigan and Wisconsin, Colorado and Idaho, Montana and other Rocky Mountain states. Canada, too. But lately I've passed up shots at more than I've killed. It's because I've come to realize that shooting a bear, especially with the help of hounds or over a bait, takes no special skills, only a reasonable amount of endurance and patience, plus pockets deep enough to pay for the hunt. But, as mentioned, I've done it myself and so I cannot begrudge those who shoot bayed or scavenging bears. It's a personal thing. It's just that now, for me at least, spot-and-stalk or calling holds more of a bear-hunting challenge.

Last fall I saw a bear on my place that I would have shot without a second thought. I was in a favorite tree stand when I heard a splashing in a finger of turbid slough water to my right. Ducks and an occasional otter or beaver sometimes swim past within sight of my stand. Whitetails, too, wade the same opaque shallows, hooves splashing an announcement of their unseen approach. So as I slowly lifted my bow from its hook and turned toward the sound, I was surprised to see a black bear—less than thirty yards away but screened by willows—emerging from the slough.

The bear stood briefly, nose up, morning sunlight highlighting the ebony coat, before shuffling away as soundless as a cloud shadow. Since I had a bear license in my pocket, I quickly lowered my bow, unbuckled my safety belt, and climbed down to follow. The bear was moving in the general direction of Dave's tree stand, perhaps two hundred yards away. And though I doubted if I could get close enough, unheard and unseen, to take a shot at the bear, I hoped at least I could push him by Dave, who was in a tree overlooking a good fence line crossing. He'd seen a bear, likely this same animal, earlier in the week. And later we'd found his scat piles on a deer trail nearby. But bears are not a common sight here, although the nearby mountains hold good numbers of blacks. And grizzlies, too.

I didn't see that bear again, and neither did Dave. But simply having a good-sized black bear wander past your deer stand is such an unexpected treat that we could not complain. Besides, we knew he was still around. Tracks, scat, and broken limbs in wild apple trees occasionally reminded us of his presence. And one dark night something spooked the horses. Badly. Whatever it was, it caused them to break through the rail fence girding their bluff-top pasture and run off into the pines. Bears have that effect on livestock. And bears undeniably fire our imaginations, too.

Like many others, I have spent countless hours trudging through darkened woodlands. Yet, truthfully, only in bear country do I so blatantly start, wince, and smile a nervous smile at the sudden cracking of a nearby branch, at the brush-breaking departure of alarmed deer, at the nerve-shattering rise of a grouse from underfoot. Automatically, unbidden, my mind turns to bears. And for a brief instant, I know the metallic taste of uneasy fear.

- Yet I do not fear bears, I insist; I merely respect them. And, intellectually, I believe that. But when I step from my tent on some unnamed Alaskan stream and see where a grizzly had walked during the night, I cannot help but eye nearby dwarf willows and devil's club with worried suspicion. And when I encounter a black bear while hunting high-country deer or elk, I still feel my heart jump at the mere sight of such a powerful, graceful, *wild* animal. That's because these are not park clowns begging for food or ignoring camera-armed tourists and roadside gawkers. These are wild bears. And you abruptly realize that you are in their backyard, at ground level, facing them on their terms.

If you do not feel a surge of adrenaline when a wild bear stops close by, turns its broad head, and fixes you with that unreadable ursine stare — a myopic gawk that could be either curiosity or contempt — you are either patently ignorant or perhaps incapable of admitting human frailty. I have no such problem.

Once, in Montana's Beaverhead backcountry, easing shadow quiet along a well-tracked elk trail, I glanced up to catch sight of a large, cinnamon-coated bear nosing in the forest duff just upslope to my right. My first thought was *grizzly*! But already my eyes were registering the absence of a shoulder hump, the dished facial profile. By the time I was able to swallow my heart, I knew it was not a silvertip but a very large, very close brown-phase black bear.

Moving in slow motion, I fished an arrow from my quiver and nocked it as the bruin slowly angled away uphill. By the time I could have released a feathered shaft, the bear was a good forty yards away, moving into a fringe of brush. Too far for me to risk an iffy shot. So when the animal crested the ridge and disappeared, I hurriedly tiptoed along the trail, which wound in the general direction taken by the bear, hoping to get ahead and intercept the unwary animal. I hadn't gone far before the hillside above me exploded in a flurry of pounding hooves and hurtling tan bodies. The bear had wandered unannounced — and unwelcome — into a herd of bedded elk. And though I stood unmoving, staring uphill, long after the brush-busting noises of the departing elk had faded, I never saw the bear again. But, in reality, once was enough. Such up-close chance meetings are rare. I knew I'd witnessed a once-in-a-lifetime wilderness scene. My memory was trophy enough.

Another time, high in the Sangre de Cristos of central Colorado, I watched from a tree stand as a medium-size black bear waddled to my bait barrel one evening, glanced briefly up at me, brazenly selected an odoriferous leg bone of a recently deceased steer, and then plopped down directly beneath my tree to gnaw on his prize. In the dusky quiet I could hear his teeth scraping on the bone. From time to time he'd peer up at me, licking his brown muzzle with an overlong pinkish tongue.

I had no intention of shooting this bear; his daddy — or perhaps his granddad — fed here, too. So I simply watched, smiling to myself, enjoying the bear's feeding antics, until early darkness fell in that timbered pocket and the bear disappeared from sight — but not from sound. I could still hear him shuffling around the barrel, occasionally cracking steer bones like seasoned firewood. And then suddenly a chill washed over me as I heard his claws scraping on the base of my tree a dozen feet below my boot soles.

Half a dozen tree steps led up to my perch. Had he merely stood on his hind legs to sniff and paw at a metal step? Or was he trying to climb my tree? Blind in the inky blackness, I could only guess. And, quite naturally, I guessed the worst.

How long I stood unmoving on that tiny rectangular platform, arrow on string, waiting, hardly daring to breathe, and straining to hear something, *anything*, I cannot say. But a lifetime later, when I finally found the courage to fumble one-handed in my pack for a flashlight and play its meager beam around the tree's base, the bear was gone. Without noise. Like black fog.

There are those people who claim bears are dark and silent woodland ghosts, materializing suddenly before them where only seconds before the forest stood empty and green. Such has not been my experience, because I have heard most approaching bears before I actually saw them: a faint cracking of underbrush, a gentle rustling in the ferns, a rock clattering away in some canyon— something that whispers "bear" even as you feel the pulse begin to snake in your temples. These have been commonplace clues to the first sign of a dark movement nearby.

I nearly air-walked from a Minnesota tree stand one still evening when a bear pushed over a rotten snag just behind me to abruptly announce his presence. And I can still picture Dave, maybe twelve at the time, racked by waves of uncontrollable body tremors when the clatter of rolling rocks in a gully just beyond our bait told us that a hungry visitor was near. Bears, real or imaginary, have a magical, eerie effect on humans.

There are would-be bear hunters I know who actually fear the appearance of a bear. They agree to hunt yet leave promising stands well before dark, hurriedly returning to some remote roadside rendezvous point, where they nervously sit in a locked vehicle waiting for their buddies or pace the roadway in a deepening dusk, pausing often to listen for the first faint whine of a pick-up vehicle and the welcome sweep of headlights through the trees.

Later, mentioning the trip, someone will ask the bear hunter, "Did you have a good time?"

"Yes," is the inevitable lie.

As for me, I know I have learned a lesson in the lonely wild places shared with bears. About the animals themselves. And about myself. It is a lesson of life, about strength and knowledge and confronting—perhaps conquering—fears, both real and imagined. Without bears, the woods we walk would be less foreboding but far emptier places.

Wilderness Memories

AMONG MY OFFICE clutter is a small, weighty, rectangular piece of gray-white petrified wood. It would make a good paperweight, I suppose, but I don't have it around for any such practical purpose. I keep it simply to remind me of a special place in my mind and heart, a wild and lonely place in the Wyoming high country where I once passed the better part of ten days in search of elk. I keep it near to remind me of what I found there. Of the bull. And more.

First of all you must understand that just getting there is no easy matter. Unless, that is, you normally ride seven to eight hours daily—covering some twenty-five up and down, beautiful but brutal miles—on a regular basis. And unless you are on intimate terms with a western saddle that looks like leather but sits like concrete. And even as you ride, growing numb from the waist down, you think of the walking to come, mostly upslope, or so it will seem, over terrain that turns legs to lead and lungs to lumps of burning larch. Still, you can't wait. Such is heeding the siren call of a true wilderness. And you understand that getting there, being there, must never be easy.

If I were a better writer, I'd paint word pictures you could see as clearly as the images I carry in my mind. But all I can do is suggest the scent of pine and the sounds of water splashing head-long through cool shadows beside the horse trail. I can mention the dark, gangly moose gaping momentarily at the passing pack string before crashing away. And there's the constant creak of sad-dles, the occasional *clack* of steel shoes on trail rocks, causing brief sparks to jump and die. And the sturdy mules, straining uphill beneath balanced panniers in fits of rude flatulence, as the miles slowly fall away. Then, finally, there's the welcome sight of dirty-white wall tents standing against the darker backdrop of tall coni-fers. We are there. Imagine all this as best you can, and you'll come close enough to joining me.

Tim and I ride from camp each day in predawn blackness, trusting the horses upward. A chill wind gnaws at our faces. An unseen limb occasionally reaches out to tug at a hat or a sleeve as we hunch blind in the cold saddles, wishing we were already on the high ridges. But soon enough we are, swinging stiffly down, loosening cinches, removing headstalls, snugging halter ropes, and leaving the patient horses behind us just as the first light of gray dawn washes stars from the eastern sky.

For a time we crouch huddled among the rocks above the timbered bowl, but the cold wind finds us anyway. We could move down into the dark trees below. But no, we agree, better to wait here, shivering and listening for the bull we know is below us, somewhere. But with morning light there is only the song of coyotes, far enough away that their first wavering cries sound like a bugling elk. It, too, is a wild song, befitting this high and lonesome place. But it is other music we seek. And at last we move down into the pines.

Walking warms us. We ease downslope, into the wind, and then upslope, and down again, and up. We make no particular effort to be quiet. Elk are noisy animals themselves, and we simply cow-call when a limb snaps beneath our boots' lugged soles or a loosened rock chatters away behind us, our reassuring chirps an all's-well signal to any wild ears marking our passing.

We rest for a time at midday, rummaging in our packs for sandwiches and snacks, sipping cool water from our canteens, and stretching out to doze in the warming sunshine like contented mountain cats. We glass feeding bighorns on the stark cliffs above us. We whisper-talk of them and the great bears and, of course, the elk that live and die up here, alone, mostly away from man and his influences. Such is the magic, the beauty, and the way of true wilderness.

Moving on at last, we work the shady benches and rocky draws, crossing old burns where cinquefoil and lupine and fox-glove now grow amid the clutter of charred skeleton trees. As evening nears, we set up by a snow-fed stream beside a grassy park that lies among a cluster of antler-slashed pines with broken limbs and weeping, sticky-wet trunks. Our occasional bugles echo and fade unanswered until, finally, in fast-fading light, we walk away and trudge up the high ridge to reclaim our horses, once again in full dark. Tomorrow we will repeat the ride and the day.

Perhaps what I liked best of all in the wilderness was the sense of timelessness I felt there. It was everywhere you looked. And listened. It was there in the ringing silence of a star-flecked night.

It was there in the wind whispers that stirred pines and caused aspen leaves to dance shimmering in sunshine so sharp sometimes it hurt your eyes. It was there in the high, rocky peaks with their shaded pockets of eternal snow beneath a sky bigger and deeper and bluer than any you've seen. It was there in the cloud shadows moving silently across timbered ridge and grassy park. It was there in the cold, sweet snowmelt that gurgled among creekbed rocks, past the gray piece of petrified wood I saw in the streamside moss and slipped into my pack as a souvenir of this time and place. And it certainly was there in the knowledge that you were breathing new air and walking faint trails more familiar to hoof and moccasin than to Vibram boot soles. It's exhilarating stuff.

One morning, just after a surprise late-summer snowfall, a bull's sudden challenge came to us even before the echoes of our own bugling faded. He was close, upset at our presence or our impudence or both. I had time only to drop to one knee, fumble an arrow from my bow quiver, and snap its fluorescent nock into place with unsteady fingers. But the bull never came.

We later found his nearby tracks easily enough. We could see where he'd walked toward us and then stood listening for a time before turning away and moving on downslope. He'd obviously had other elk business on his mind this day and was satisfied to let us off with a stern warning. My heart was still thudding as we walked away with only the memory of his screaming challenge— and pants wet from the knees down after crouching in the heavy snow. At the moment, that was enough.

I still carry memories of the camp coming awake and going to sleep in darkness. Of the scratch of tent fly zippers, the clank of cast-iron lids, the rasp of matches, the hiss of Coleman lanterns. You burrow deeper in your warm bag, listening to the muffled muttering of your tentmate, waiting for the stove to chase away the worst of the chill before worming out of downy comfort into cold camouflage and stiff boots. The tiredness in your legs and feet reminds you of the miles already walked. But by the time you've quickly dressed and made your way to the cook tent you're ready, even eager. Again. After all, *this* could be the day. And if not today, tomorrow for sure. The bulls have to start bugling sometime.

Around the lamplit table, over eggs and sausage and griddle cakes and fresh-baked bread, cold juice and hot coffee, you talk of yesterday's almosts and today's maybes. Amid boasting and banter mingled with the smells of breakfast and wood smoke, you begin another day. Meanwhile, the wranglers ride out to find the belled horses and, shouting and swearing, drive them back from the pasture through darkness to the corral. Soon ours are saddled and tied waiting, breath forming ghosts in yellow lantern light. We again grab packs and bugles and bows and begin another day. In darkness.

Our day ends in darkness, as well. Late. We return tired, the campfire glow a welcoming beacon winking at us through the pines. Supper is waiting, good grub the cooks have worked at. We wash hurriedly and eat hungrily, for the most part quieter than at breakfast, dutifully recounting who had seen and heard what. But the long day has dulled us, and soon we drift off to our tents and waiting cots. Snuggling in sleeping bags, hoping tomorrow will bring the bugling of bulls, we sleep until the sudden ripping of our tent zipper rouses us to renew the now-familiar routine.

And then comes the day, just before noon, when *the* bull answers our tentative bugling. He is at least two drainages away, but from where we sit among the jumble of boulders, his wavering, flutelike warning drifts to us through the crisp air as clearly as the distant calling of cathedral bells. Above the timbered bowl, we stand for a moment, looking and listening across the green treetops before bugling again. When he answers, we nod and step off the ridge line, slip-sliding down the cliff face in ankle-deep loose dirt and stones.

We rock-hop a rushing stream and claw our way up into the timber, hurrying along a tracked game trail until the ground falls away to our left. We again plunge downslope, digging in our heels and riding small scree avalanches into the next basin. And then we fight our way upward again, sweat stinging our eyes, lungs aflame, until we reach the bench and stop, gasping, to look and listen.

I move ahead a dozen paces and kneel beside a deadfall. Tim bugles behind me. The bull answers just ahead. I pull an arrow free and snap it on the string. Tim bugles again, but when the bull answers he is moving away.

I jam the arrow back into the quiver even as I clamber to my feet. Another footrace. Sprinting among the pine trees, dodging low-hanging branches, and hurdling blowdowns. Down and across a sunny, boulder-strewn chute. Up into the cool trees beyond. Finding another deadfall hiding spot even as Tim bugles again.

This time the bull's scream is close. Indignant at being pushed, he is just ahead. Defiant. Angry. By the time I nock my arrow for the third time, I can hear brush breaking uphill to my left. Dark legs appear, moving. A heavy, ivory-tipped rack floats toward me, somehow disembodied. He is thirty yards away and closing.

God, I think, awestruck, *the size, the beauty of him!*

Still he moves toward me, head-on, as noiseless now as a tan shadow. Drifting downslope, passing behind a pine at twenty yards, he doesn't see me come to full draw, hear my thudding heart, sense me near. He only knows the rival bull is close, a threat to his cows waiting in the timber above. On he stalks. Closer. Closer.

Turn, I pray, *please turn!*

And at last, as if by my will alone, he does turn. Over my bow hand I watch the bull ghosting past, broadside, huge yet silent, striding, until my arrow's red and yellow fletching appears against his side, tight behind the shoulder, just where I willed it to fly.

He spins and crashes through a deadfall graveyard, down into the rocky chute. There he stands briefly in brilliant midday sunshine, the spreading crimson patch glistening. Then slowly he walks off into the shade beyond, perhaps wondering at the unseen bull that had somehow hooked and hurt him. When he is out of sight I walk weak-kneed to where his hooves tore the forest duff as my arrow buried itself deep in his lungs. It is but a dozen short steps. My hands are still trembling as Tim joins me. We sit together, whispering, waiting for the sharp steel to do its work.

I could speak of the short tracking job, the long hours of field dressing, skinning, packing, caping. Of the long ride out, the pack mules loaded with fresh, cool meat and the antlers of a wilderness monarch I'd met and can never forget. I dutifully record such things in my notebook, penciling times and dates and facts that over the years will fade like old photos. They're there to help others who later might read my words and try to imagine what it was like.

For me, though, there is no true way — or need — to capture on paper what in reality cannot be captured. Memories. I need only to glimpse the piece of petrified wood resting amid my office's eternal clutter to pause and relive the mystery of the Wyoming wilderness, to recall the hunt, the stalk, the shot, and so much more. And each time I see the wood-turned-stone, touch its waterworn smoothness, lift its surprising heft in my fingers, I dream of returning.

The elk are still up there. And the sheep. And the great bears. Along with a part of my soul I left to cry for those who will never walk a wilderness trail.

Ol' Big and Ugly

I COULD HEAR the spooked muley buck coming a long time before I saw him. And once you've heard it, there is absolutely no mistaking the ground-jarring, brush-busting gallop of a big mule deer crashing through mountain mahogany and oak brush. It's a memorable sound that has always set my pulse to pounding. This time was no exception.

It was early September, and I was standing smack in the middle of a well-used game trail near the bottom of a cup-shaped aspen pocket. The muley was smashing through the brush on the hillside directly above me, coming closer with every bound. The timber in front of me was fairly open. Getting a shot would not be a problem. The problem would be, as always, getting a *good* shot. The thought of shooting a galloping buck head-on at point-blank range held no appeal for me. Neither did trying to explain how I came to have heart-shaped hoofprints in my camouflaged clothing.

Suddenly the big buck burst into the open, already sleek and gray although it was the early season, when most muleys are still red coated and summertime fat. His high, velvety rack carried at least four points to a side. A nice buck, I thought, planting my feet and raising my bow.

But something was wrong. The onrushing buck appeared to be breathing fire. Streaks of crimson stained his flaring nostrils and his outstretched neck. My bow was held at half draw, forgotten. I could merely gape as the specter veered sharply to the left. Only then did I see the broken shaft protruding from the deer's rib cage. Abruptly everything I was witnessing made perfect sense.

Jack, my hunting partner, later explained how he had seen several deer moving through the trees below him shortly after he had slipped into the shadowy aspen pocket. Then a four-by-four buck plodded slowly uphill, stopping to stand quartering away just beyond a wind-felled snag thirty-five yards from where Jack stood watching. An instant later Jack's arrow threaded its way between two of the deadfall's limbs and buried itself in the muley's chest. We soon found that buck, with Jack's broken shaft still protruding from its side, lying in a small opening in the brush near the edge of the aspen pocket.

That Colorado hunt was made in the late 1960s. It wasn't the first trip Jack and I took together. It wouldn't be the last. But it was typical of the adventures two good friends can experience together in the outdoors. And if your best memories of times afield or afloat are crowded with such vivid and unforgettable shared moments, you already understand why someone like Jack is so important. Some things simply are meant to be shared. And sharing them with someone special always enhances both the experience and the memory.

I affectionately called Jack "Ol' Big and Ugly." I used to tell him he wasn't much to look at on the hoof, especially in some hunting camp beneath a week's worth of steel-wool stubble and surrounded by a cloud of blue smoke from one of his toxic, foul-scented cigars. But I never meant it, of course. It was simply because he was a friend and sometimes friends good-naturedly tag each other with nicknames that may fit a momentary occasion, then somehow stick. That's the way it happened with Jack and me. I can't write down what Jack mostly called me because I know women and kids might read this book. But I never took offense. Neither did he.

Like me, Ol' Big and Ugly stood an inch or two over six feet. But while I was a lanky two hundred pounds, Jack was spindly legged and barrel chested—like the square-jawed, bare-knuckle brawlers you see in those grainy fight films showing Sullivan or Corbett or some such pugilist—and he probably outweighed me by a good forty or fifty pounds. He had this shock of thick, dark hair when we first met; later on it became streaked with gray but unlike mine didn't thin much. He wore eyeglasses and an Ernest Borgnine smile most times, and I guess he had ten or twelve years on me. But despite our age difference, or perhaps because of it, we hit it off right from the start. And some of my best memories of big game hunts recall times Jack and I spent together.

Rudy and Noel and all my other boyhood friends were different. I grew up with them, went through school with them, learned about hunting with them. We inherited each other as hunting partners, much the same way I took to hunting with my nephews, Sonny and Ron, and the rest of my family. Jack was the first person I later met and hunted with by choice. The fact was, I simply enjoyed being with the man.

Appropriately enough, we met at an archery range just outside

Princeton, Indiana, in the early 1960s. And although we plinked chucks in the spring and fox squirrels in the late summer, our passion for bows and bucks occupied most of our serious hunting time together. And from the overgrown strip mine pits of nearby Hoosierland whitetail haunts, it was a long but natural step to head beyond the Wabash to other big game and other challenges. In time, season after season, the Book Cliffs of Colorado and Utah came to pull us like steel shavings to a magnet.

Back then you could legally take one deer in Colorado and two in Utah, starting in mid-August, a full month and a half before the Indiana bow season opened. Each year we'd hear the mountains calling, kiss Midge and Janet and our kids goodbye, and point Jack's pickup or my station wagon—loaded to the gunwales with hunting gear—toward the setting sun. More often than not we'd be back in a couple of weeks with enough stories and western venison to last us until the following season rolled around.

The thing about Ol' Big and Ugly was that he was fun to be with. And whenever I filled my tag, he was as happy as if it had been his arrow that put the buck down. Reverse things and I honestly felt the same way. And to my way of thinking, that says something for the kind of relationship we shared. To me, that's the true test of any hunting friendship: mutual enjoyment and admiration without the slightest hint of jealousy.

Seems some folks can't resist turning hunting into a competition, a contest they have to win in order to achieve satisfaction. I pity them. Being the first to limit out or to tag the biggest buck never meant all that much to Jack or me. Neither did getting skunked. Again, it's the hunting and not the killing that should matter most. Ethics. Tradition. Fairness. Respect. Sharing. These are, ideally, what hunting is all about. Folks who have to have blood on their hands before they consider their hunt successful have a warped sense of values.

Bowhunting, by its nature, is pretty much a difficult, solitary sport. Two people always make twice the noise, doubling its degree of difficulty. And when getting close enough for a good shot at unalarmed game is your goal, it's best accomplished alone. But that fact doesn't preclude the benefits of sharing a camp with a friend or friends. After a day spent still-hunting or stalking or sitting on some likely stand, almost any hunter can find comfort and release in friendly companionship. And no one I know will argue the benefit of traveling to and from some local or distant hunting area in the company of a good friend. Nothing I've found can shorten long miles faster, heighten the anticipation quicker, or make recent success seem sweeter than sharing travel time with a friend. Conversely, nothing can create more tension, sour a relationship, or spoil a hunt faster than a crotchety companion whose complaining affects everyone involved. Bad memories, like bad coffee, leave an unpleasant, bitter taste and turn moments meant to be savored into times best forgotten.

That's why Jack—and all special people like him—are true treasures, rare and priceless. Once discovered, they enrich your life as long as there are shared moments or lingering memories of those times spent together.

Ol' Big and Ugly retired some time back. And I guess I've invited him out to my place half a dozen times since. But Indiana is a long way from Montana. Besides, Midge has been ailing and Jack's bursitis has been acting up, so they pretty much stay close to home and their four girls, all grown women now, who look after them.

I understand. But still, that doesn't prevent me from wanting one more hunt together, from being admittedly selfish. Because even though it's been a long time now since our last shared hunt, I know nothing really has changed between us over the years. I know him. He knows me. Some things simply do not change.

Even today, hunting my place alone, I do not hear a soft bird whistle without coming alert, believing for an instant it is Jack's familiar signal to me that a buck is moving my way. And there are times when I'm still-hunting and see a shadow move somewhere uphill that I stop and stare, half expecting to see Jack step into the open, nod, smile, and silently move on, paralleling me the way he's done a hundred times. Such is the familiar teamwork of hunters, of friends.

Ol' Big and Ugly wasn't much of a camp cook. His beer and bologna breakfasts held little appeal for me, unless I was unaccountably ravenous. But I will admit that he did make a passable peanut butter and jelly sandwich. And he'd share the last drink from his canteen or his last dollar to pay for his share of the gas on a trip home from hunting camp. And it's true he rarely complained — except to sleepily protest when I'd chuck a pillow his way in the middle of the night to briefly stop his fits of infernal, cabin-shaking snoring (a venial camp sin he always indignantly denied committing).

The last time I saw Jack was in the cluttered little archery shop he ran for years in the converted garage beside his house just east of Princeton. The shop's walls are littered with a lifetime of hunting mementos. Photos. Game mounts. Trophies.

A left-turn shoulder mount of the mortally wounded Colorado buck that nearly trampled me is there, the two pieces of Jack's broken arrow shaft resting in its antler tines. The rack of my first muley is hanging there, too, along with antlers of an Illinois eight-pointer I shot down in Pope County while I was still in school. Our smiling faces, framed and frozen forever in time by the clicking of a camera, are eternally young. Or at least younger. And the memories they evoke are good ones.

Ol' Big and Ugly never could resist reminding me of that time I was almost trampled by his buck. It always was the opening I'd been waiting for. I would ask if he remembered one of our last hunts together.

It was early November, one of those cool and misty fall afternoons when the woods are whisper quiet and whitetail bucks are on the move. I put Jack in my favorite oak tree stand and then climbed into a stand in a hickory tree maybe a hundred yards away. During the night or early morning a buck had opened a scrape twenty-five yards away from the shagbark, and I was hoping he'd return to freshen it after a day of light rain.

I hadn't much more than settled down to wait when I spotted a basket-racked buck walking uphill behind me. He moved directly to the scrape and began raking his antlers on a skinny sapling. I slowly stood and turned, but I carelessly scraped my bow's lower limb on the tree as I shifted into shooting position. The buck jerked alert and stared my way for a full minute or more. Finally satisfied, he lowered his head again to resume working over the helpless sapling.

Ol' Big and Ugly always smiled at this point in my story,

taking his cue. "I'm sitting in this big white oak tree near the edge of a clearing. The wet leaves below are churned up where the deer have been feeding on acorns. I'm sitting and thinking about deer when all of a sudden I hear one running my way.

"I look up and here comes this buck, right at me. I stand up and get ready to shoot. Then all at once I see this arrow sticking out right behind its left shoulder. And I know my hunting buddy has done it to me again. I'm only thankful I was in that tree. Otherwise I might have had to explain how I came to be run down by this wounded buck."

Like someone once said, Jack, what goes around comes around. I don't know about you, but I wouldn't have it any other way.

Have You Ever...?

THE THING I notice most about living in the West is the honesty of the people. Not that there aren't honest people everywhere. There are. It's just that you can't usually find whole coveys of them. Back where I come from they're mostly singles and doubles.

Westerners are generally a friendly lot, too. And most are close to the land, which probably makes a big difference in their outlook on life. If they don't hunt and fish—which most do—they ski or snowmobile or kayak or canoe or backpack or rock-climb or hang glide or ride horseback or whatever's outdoorsy and grabs their interest at the time. Sure, some golf and play tennis and such, but you can do that anywhere. In the West, it's in to be out-of-doors.

Me, I like the simple fact I can go to town or out to eat with Janet and friends without having to change out of my jeans and boots and flannel shirt. And I can grow a salt-and-pepper beard and let my thinning hair creep down over my collar without attracting disapproving stares from strangers.

I've walked into airport and motel lobbies in Great Falls, Cody, Casper, Butte, and Grand Junction wearing dirty camouflage and a week's growth of whiskers—and probably smelling like a bottle of spilled buck scent—and I've still rated a smile and a "Sir" from the friendly person behind the counter. Try that in Indianapolis sometime.

Westerners, I've come to discover, move at a much slower pace than eastern and midwestern folk. And when a delivery or repairman is supposed to be there by noon Friday, there's an inherent "maybe" that goes with that commitment. After all, they probably didn't say *which* Friday.

Living in the West does remind me of growing up in a small Illinois town in one respect: the nearness to the country. Except that here the country is just outside your back door. And you aren't really surprised when you drive up your rutted lane to see half a dozen deer in the pine shadows behind the hay barn—and one's a decent four-by-four. Or when you glance out across the yard during lunch and see Merriam's turkeys or ruffed grouse picking along the rail fence. Or when the geese on the river waken you at daybreak on a spring morning. Or when you're filling the wood bin and look up to see a bald eagle resting in the big cottonwood below the bluff. You don't see such sights in the cities.

Have you ever wanted these sights and sounds for yourself? If so, you understand what it is I'm saying here about the West. If so, you know why I feel the way I do about the West. But it's not for everyone. And I thank God for that.

I came to the West for the first time when I was a few months old, or so I've been told. I made it back just about every year since, visiting kinfolk in Wichita, Pueblo, and Cheyenne. Old photo albums overflow with snapshots of a skinny, freckled kid squinting at the camera from a lot of western locales. A favorite shows me grinning from the back of a buckin' bronc photo prop like some real-life rodeo cowboy.

My Aunt Ruth, who today lives only in family memories and faded snapshots, lived on a Colorado ranch. I rode my first horse there, when Aunt Ruth saddled and boosted me onto a gentle, one-eyed buckskin gelding. Old Buck plodded down the lane behind the barn, past the stock-tank embankment where my uncle and the hired hand hid when shooting autumn ducks, and out into the sage and bunchgrass beyond, taking me and my smile along for the ride. But later that same day I trudged back, leading Buck, chagrined and defeated. Short in the britches, I'd been unable to remount after climbing down to check out some coyote tracks in the prairie dust. Still, I'm forever smiling in the pictures of me astride that aged buckskin.

Buck was the first horse to throw me, too. That year, or maybe the next, I was riding in the pasture in front of Aunt Ruth's house when several neighborhood dogs came yapping our way to nip at Old Buck's plodding unshod hooves. That sent him into the stiff-legged trot all beginning riders dread. I hung on to the horn as long as I could, but Buck's gait and gravity soon combined to dump me unceremoniously in the Colorado dust. Only my pride was bruised. And I've taken worse spills since.

Once, in Colorado, I was riding on one of John Lamicq's sorrels during a mid-June bear hunt above his Roan Creek camp. I had my hooded St. Charles back quiver, with its full complement of a dozen arrows, looped over the saddlehorn. As the mare passed close by a manzanita bush, a scraggly limb caught and bent the quiver's padded metal base.

Well, when that first aluminum arrow clattered against the

rocky ground, the sorrel promptly laid back its ears and twisted its head around to see what the racket was. About then a couple more arrows fell out, and that mare started prancing uphill, sidestepping the racket yet causing still more arrows to rattle out. I threw my Black Widow bow into a passing bush and bailed off that bucking bronc. On the downhill side.

John came rushing over all worried and wide-eyed, asking if I was all right. I was. We had a nervous laugh about it before we set about retrieving my recurve and metal arrows, which were strewn for thirty yards down the mountainside. John also passed along a bit of advice I try to remember each time I mount up. "Next time you get bucked off a horse," he said, "try to land on the *uphill* side. That way you don't have so far to fall."

I have horses of my own these days. My favorite is Ric — short for Ricochet — a leggy paint gelding with a congenial disposition that suits me just fine. He still shies when a grouse whirs out from under his hooves. And he sunfished with me once after straddling a hidden whitetail fawn that burst bleating from a reed-grass clump between his legs. But I didn't blame him. It scared me, too.

Horses, of course, are a part of the West. I don't remember Tom and Tony, but I grew up with Roy and Trigger, Gene and Champion, and other heroes of the Saturday matinees. Twenty cents got you three color cartoons, a serial, and the feature Western we all came to see. Johnny Mack Brown, Charles Starrett — as the Durango Kid, of course — Whip Wilson, Bill Boyd as Hopalong Cassidy, and Lash LaRue, among other celluloid cowboys, rode into my life each week. And forever.

I've known some real cowboys, too. Hard men with rough hands, leather-lined faces, and — mostly — honest-to-God bowed legs, scruffy sweat-stained hats, old down-at-the-heel boots, dirty denim jeans with frayed cuffs and snuff-can rings worn into one hip pocket, faded bandannas, wash-thinned print shirts with at least one button missing, and roll-your-own makings causing one flapped pocket to bulge.

Theirs is mostly a hard and lonely life. I've read their names and thoughts and dreams in aspen carvings that, when discovered on some hike or hunt, remind us anew of their presence and passing. And sometimes I sit for a time where they once sat and thought and felt and maybe wondered about living and dying and such. Up here, in out-of-the-way places, a man can be full of himself until the icy winking of a million stars fills the night sky with a piquant reminder of his insignificance and mortality.

Many of the guides and outfitters I've come to know over the years are cowboys, too, most knowing more about bucks and bulls than business, and caring more about some keen-nosed strike hound or hardy horse than they do about many of the people in their lives. Few are rich, or even well off, in a materialistic sense; however, most have everything they need, including the patient understanding of some fine helpmate who at times does without company and comfort, who isn't above pitching in to work elbow to elbow with her man through calving season or hunting camp chores. And who still can manage a friendly smile and firm handshake for yet another visiting dude willing to buy her husband's time and talents.

Westerners, for the most part, are more interested in meat on the table and in the freezer than in horns on the wall. That's why they develop a talent for braking the pickup and reaching for the rifle in the rear-window gun rack all in the same motion. And that's why tags bearing the names of nonshooting womenfolk and youngsters get filled each season. Wild meat once fed the West, and even today some families have meat on the table mostly because of a rock-steady aim and nature's bounty.

These same folks generally don't have much use for government meddling of any sort, or the government itself, for that matter. And the mere mention of any federal agency gives rise to expletives and has likely caused the breaking of the "cussing" commandment more than any other reason.

And in a land where many folks make their living off what grows on and what lies under the earth, there's not a lot of patience with people who would put nature ahead of earning a livelihood. Wilderness is wonderful, most westerners admit, but you can't eat trees and aesthetics alone don't pay the bills. And when push comes to shove, they forgo unspoiled scenery in favor of steady employment.

Theirs can be a hard life in a hard land. Always has been. Always will be. So before judging them, you have to have a go at understanding them or you'll apply back East logic to them and their ways, which is easy but probably not fair.

And before you quit your tiresome job and eagerly pack your bags to set off and join those of us who live in the West, you need to take a long look at why there aren't more of us out here. True, it's a great place to live. But mostly it's not a great place to make a living. Which keeps it special for those who can.

I can't make any claims to being a true westerner, but I do fit in here simply because I don't stand out. And although I admit my view is idyllic, I do share many of the feelings that westerners have about their region and way of life.

For instance, like many, I enjoy going for a walk after a rain just to smell the sage or the fresh-washed scent of pines.

I think bear grass is as pleasing to the eye as huckleberries are to the palate.

I agree with those who believe the Indian paintbrush should be the West's official flower.

I do believe a pickup can be a good family vehicle.

I'd rather listen to Willie Nelson and Alabama than Aerosmith and Phil Collins any day. And Reba McEntire can sing Madonna under the table anytime, anyplace.

I always wear my jeans over my boots but respect those who prefer to tuck theirs inside.

I now count the points on just one side of a buck's or a bull's rack when telling how big he was.

I still have some shirts that button, but most of them snap.

I now prefer big belt buckles and bolo ties.

I cannot hear the word *gold* without thinking of sunlight shimmering on a patch of September quaking aspen.

I can hear the word *cold* and have half a dozen handy anecdotes about last winter's cold snap or getting caught in a ground blizzard that time we were elk hunting in the Beaverhead.

I now can stand downwind from a horse pasture or feedlot and tell the difference. By smell alone.

I also believe people who cut the throats of deer they've just shot are plumb dumb.

I, too, call the bear bells worn by backpackers in grizzly country "dinner bells."

I know for a fact that fresh-caught trout tastes better cooked over an open fire than in the fanciest restaurant on earth.

I will always feel sorry for people who drive through Yellowstone or Glacier and think they've had a wilderness experience.

In fact, I feel sorry for everybody who lives in a city—or a town with more than a dozen streets—but, again, I thank God it's so hard to make a living in the West because it's already crowded enough.

Finally, I understand why almost anyone who's stood on a mountain at night, staring up at the stars, believes there's a God behind it all.

Have you ever? I have. And I do.

Heroes

I LIKE TO hear Willie singing that his heroes have always been cowboys. Each time that particular ballad comes on the radio, I cannot help but pause, listen to his words, and think about my own heroes—cowboys and otherwise—who have made some real difference in my life. Without heroes, I'm convinced, all of us would be poorer for having passed through this business called life without benefit of admiring, respecting, or emulating someone special.

My first hero, I suppose, was my dad. He introduced me to hunting and fishing when I wasn't as big as old Doc Couch's shotgun. He let me tag along with him down by the Bonpas and carry the fox squirrels or cottontails he shot for Sunday dinner. Once he even let me carry the heavy twelve-gauge—empty, of course—and he didn't even yell at me when I slipped while crossing a muddy field and jammed the muzzle into the mire. Instead, he patiently took the occasion to show me how to take the gun apart and remove the mud. He explained why you can't just shoot the gumbo out of the barrel and how dangerous it is to pull the trigger on any firearm with a blocked barrel.

Dad also taught me how to bait a hook with a fat, red night crawler, how to spit on it for luck, how to cast a line, and then how to wait until the bobber had gone all the way under before firmly setting the hook. He showed me how to scale a bluegill and skin a catfish. And though I didn't realize it at the time, every day we were together in some bottomland weed patch or woodlot or standing shoulder to hip beside some murky farm pond, he was planting seeds that would grow and blossom each season for as long as I lived.

I probably never thought of Dad as a hero back then. But I do now. And he was.

Mom was another kind of hero, because it was she who first introduced me to literary heroes like Robinson Crusoe, Robin Hood, and *Les Trois Mousquetaires*, not to mention Tom and Huck and other rascally boys I could more easily identify with. She read me a chapter every day just before bedtime, filling my mind and my dreams with exciting adventures and vivid images of far-away places. And after I learned to read the words for myself, Mom made sure no birthday or Christmas passed without one or more wrapped books among my presents. In short, she gave me an early and lasting love for the written word. And it was Mom, I realize now, who set my life on its inexorable course, gently guiding me toward a career as a writer and editor. It was Mom who made me an eternal admirer of all those skillful wordcrafters whose talent, when shared, contains the capacity to reach out and touch readers everywhere.

Mr. Kolb, a neighbor who lived in a white frame house at the top of the Cedar Street hill, was my first nonfamily hunting hero. Not only did he fill his limit of bushytails with amazing regularity, but he also took the time to patiently show a gangly, freckled boy how to skin a fox squirrel without getting hair on the meat and how simple it is to use spit and an Arkansas stone to put a shaving-sharp edge on a pocketknife blade. Heady stuff guaranteed to impress adventurous young friends if not instinctively protective mothers.

Besides hunting, for me there was always off-season baseball, the game of boyhood heroes. A left-handed pitcher/outfielder, Dad had played semipro ball in Wichita back in the 1930s and always did what he could to instill a love of the game in his only son. It was an easy chore.

Little League, Pony, Colt, Legion, and high school ball, all the way to college, I played and, like millions of dreamers, imagined making it to the majors someday. The nearest big-league park was in Saint Louis, and I grew up listening to Harry Caray and watching the Redbirds, even though I wasn't really a Cardinals fan. My heroes were Musial and Mays, Aaron and Mathews, Snider and Clemente—National Leaguers all. And mostly outfielders, like me, although Eddie played third and Stan, late in his career, first base.

Youthful dreams die. Realism sets in with the realization that a strong arm isn't enough, that you're a step or two slow, and your front foot has a mind of its own when a major-league curve heads your way. But the heroes remain. Some you remember forever.

I once spent three days with Hank Aaron, thanks to a writing job. By talking to the man, watching him with people like you and me, I gained a new perspective. This was after Babe's record had fallen and Hank's playing days had ended, when he was touring and pushing products and filling young heads with dreams of success in baseball and beyond. What I saw up close was a man, not just a hero. And what I admired most was the way he put on a game face, no matter how long the demanding day had been. He always smiled and shook hands and signed pictures and baseballs, giving a small something back to the people, his people.

"It's a job and it gets tiresome," he once said as we drove between appearances. "But I don't mind. The fans help keep the memories alive."

The only American Leaguer I ever spent time with was Brooks Robinson. Parking my old clunker, I drove the family station wagon to the airport to pick him up. We mostly talked about hunting and fishing instead of baseball, and I soon knew he was the sort who wouldn't have cared a whit about the car you drove. He talked about growing up down in Arkansas, asked about local hunting and fishing opportunities, and met his admiring fans with a friendly smile and handshake as routinely as he'd field a screaming hot corner one-hopper back on that hard-packed Baltimore infield.

I was surprised to note that one of baseball's best third basemen ever, who batted and threw righty, signed autographs left-handed. And in my mind I can see him swinging on a covey rise as easily as on a darting slider—with equal results. I could even forgive Brooks Robinson for playing in the American League; he was one of the most unassuming heroes anyone could meet.

Dad, shortly before he died, met Don Mattingly. To a lifelong Yankee fan like Dad, the meeting was special. Dad saw Mattingly in an Evansville mall one winter day, marched right over, introduced himself, and told the Yankee infielder he admired him as a player and wanted to wish the Yanks well in the 1990s. Mattingly graciously shook Dad's hand and even signed a piece of paper for him, briefly turning a dying eighty-four-year-old man into a kid again. Heroes have that power, you know.

Inspired by reading L'Amour, thrilled by sharing the adventures of his heroes—notably those of the Sackett clan—I wrote and sold my first Western short story in 1959. It was called "Trouble at Little Spring" and its unlikely hero was a crippled wrangler who thwarted a stage depot robbery. Come to think of it, a lot of my heroes have always been cowboys.

But hunting and fishing have their heroes, too. Reading Ruark and Hemingway, O'Connor and Buckingham, Bear and Hill, Thompson and Pope, and all of the others who inspire and fascinate so many of us, I shared their experiences while living my own. And over the years, as I came to appreciate their literary legacy, I made a vow to offer thanks by leaving others a gift of my own.

It was Roy Hoff, the editor/founder of *Archery* magazine, who first published and encouraged my initial nonfiction efforts in the mid-1960s. Although we didn't meet until the early 1970s, we grew to know each other well through countless telephone conversations and exchanges of correspondence. By the time we met in Roy's native Colorado, I wasn't facing a hero for the first time; I was finally meeting an old friend.

Roy wasn't a great writer or editor, I suppose. But to me he was a genuine hero, a man who started with an idea for a publication and who eventually, once his dream became reality, touched thousands. Thanks to him and what he demonstrated could be accomplished by purposeful dedication, dogged determination, and hard but honest work, I was inspired to trail in his editorial footsteps.

The last time I spent with him was back in Ohio in '78 at his induction into the Archery Hall of Fame. We had a good talk, and I thanked him for everything he'd done for me and for bowhunting. He modestly brushed aside my compliments, commenting, "I'm no hero. I'm just a man who does what he thinks is right and hopes things won't turn out wrong."

Fred Bear was always a hero to me, too. I first met him in Denver in 1973. I last saw him in Tulsa in 1988, about a year before he died. In between, we exchanged letters and telephone calls, crossing trails occasionally although we never found time to hunt together. And even though I never got to know him as well as I'd have liked, I grew to respect what he accomplished and how he handled the responsibility of fame.

· I remember Bear as a hardheaded Dutchman who was by-God stubborn but thrived on action and attention. No matter how tired he was or how ill he became, I never saw him turn down a request for a photo or an autograph. Better than most, he understood his obligation to set a good example for those who looked up to him.

Friends of mine from Wyoming once found his name carved in an aged aspen near where he'd shot an elk. They snapped a picture of the carving and sent it to me to determine if it was authentic. I asked Fred about it. He hemmed and hawed for a time before finally owning up to the signature.

"I gotta be careful," he confided. "I've only done that a couple of times. I don't want people thinking I go around defacing public property on national forest lands by carving my name on trees. That wouldn't look so good."

Looking good is something most heroes don't have to worry about, at least to their admirers. To most they can do no wrong. And even if on occasion they do something disappointing, forgiveness usually isn't that hard to come by. All it takes is asking. Or time. Most often that's enough.

Time, especially, is what it takes to enhance the memories of special people. The longer your life, the more you are certain to be affected by heroes, and the more likely you are to become a hero yourself. Age carries with it certain entitlements and obligations. Over time, young people—most notably sons, daughters, and grandchildren, although neighborhood youngsters do nicely, too—have a way of attaching themselves to adults who pay attention to them, actually listen to them, and help make growing up a bit more meaningful.

That's why today I take special pleasure in helping some eager boy or girl get started on the right foot in the outdoors. Whether it's showing how to lay down a bunt, squeeze a trigger, bait a hook, or find a nocking point, I need only to be asked and given the chance.

You can't force it, of course. But you can make it as interesting as possible in order to create curiosity. You can care enough to be patient, to encourage effort. And you can help, more than you may know, simply by being there.

This is nothing new. It is nothing but common sense. But there are times when people need to be reminded what it was like to be young, to be alive with enthusiasm for the sheer joy of living from one day to the next and spending time with someone special. A hero, real or imagined.

My fervent hope is that come the opening day of next fishing or hunting season, or at some point in between, you and I will share the experience of field, woods, or water with an acquaintance, newly met or otherwise. And the look in those large, eager eyes, the quickness in his or her new-booted step, the crisp rustling of new-bought clothing, the shortness of breath, and the trembling of fingers fumbling with a reel's drag or a firearm's safety will be reward enough for our investment of time.

At such moments, there is no need for words. To the hero in all of us, the sharing—the simple act of being out there, together—is truly all that matters.

Little Things

I TOLERATE THE colony of gophers living in the horse pasture as they likewise tolerate me. I used to shoot some each year, but the red foxes—hunting with their annual litter of kits born in a den along the bluff overlooking Goodrich Bayou—always took a higher toll. And owls and hawks ghosting from the shadowy pines on whisper-quiet wings claimed even more. These artful, uncaring killers kept the gophers from overrunning the place; the token payment I exacted—and my reason for quitting—were personal matters.

I shot my last gopher this past spring. He was standing at the burrow mouth when my hunting arrow took him through the chest at just over thirty yards. Pulling the stained shaft free, I wiped his blood on the green grass and walked away. "No more," I said aloud. Killing little things to practice for killing bigger things suddenly held no appeal for me.

Dave and certain friends still stalk my horse pasture and shoot gophers. And at times I join them. They joke and call me a "gopher guide." I do not mind. I have been called worse. I am there simply because I enjoy their company. And because I have imposed certain rules they must follow in order to hunt.

Bows only, for one. No rimfire .22s in the pasture. Not just because of the noise and the horses and the off chance of a ricochet; it's just my rule, my personal idea of fairness. Of right and wrong.

No shots under twenty-five yards. Too easy, mostly. And no fair knowing exact distances as happens when you toe the stake at a club practice range. So, it goes without saying that rangefinders are verboten. Again, horse-pasture gopher shooting is strictly my interpretation of fair chase. Accept that fact and you're welcome to join us. Argue any of the points and you can find your own horse pasture and make up your own rules.

We'll begin the day by walking down the two-track lane to the stables and tack room, past the machine shed where I store split lodgepole and larch firewood instead of ranch implements. We can open the gate or climb the rail fence by the hay shed. Your choice. Either way, the gophers will hear or see us before we step into the pasture, and their curt whistling chirps will fill the morning air like a bird chorus in the near distance. You can see a few scurrying between holes, others standing erect like picket pins, jerking perceptibly with each scolding peep. Ric, D.J., Mat, and the other horses look up from their grazing on a nearby grassy hillside, decide we're about business not affecting them, and lower their heads again.

Growing up in southeastern Illinois, I cut my small game teeth on groundhogs, not gophers. Walking the fence lines and rails of Wabash County, I carried a scoped .22 or a hunting bow, making a lot of farmers happy and a lot of groundhogs dead. One summer I shot sixty-some of the crop-raiding critters on three farms. I did it at the request of the busy farmers, who in return for my pest control gladly granted permission to later hunt their same fields and woodlots for squirrels, rabbits, and birds.

"Kill 'em all!" one landowner urged, pointing to a soybean field slowly succumbing to daily raids by dozens of the voracious rodents.

I didn't, of course, although I did thin out the resident crop somewhat and—I suppose—save a few bushels of soybeans in the process. But I left some for "seed," too, just the way I do when I consciously avoid overshooting a covey of bobwhites or some hardwood patch teeming with fox squirrels. Killing 'em all may make emotional sense to landowners at times; however, it also makes for a lot of empty, idle tomorrows for us hunters.

Groundhogs are a lot bigger than gophers. Standing erect in the fresh dirt at the mouths of their burrows, with their grizzled, ursine appearance, they remind me of miniature bruins. And while a lot of varmint hunters enjoy long-range gunning, I never much cared for simply centering the cross hairs and touching off a round at some distant target in the clover. It's much too impersonal for my taste; your tools do all the work. Give me still-hunting or spot-and-stalk anytime.

Time was when killing was the thing, too. We used to hide in the Baird henhouse across from St. Mary's Cemetery and ambush spatzies attracted to the grain scattered daily in the chicken yard. Up close, a BB from a Red Ryder air rifle can end the life of a sparrow as certainly as a .222 Swift can drop a remote groundhog. Bird and beast, both instantly dead with the squeeze of a trigger.

We used to walk the shaded creek banks, too, sniping at turtles sunning themselves on logs in or near the water's edge. The occasional cracks of .22s marked our progress along wooded waterways. We missed far more than we hit, but at times there would be a hollow plop and a lolling turtle would cartwheel into the mud, blood trickling from its ruined shell.

At the time, I never gave a second thought to using living targets for practice. It wasn't until years later, reading words written in the century after Christ's death—by the Greek biographer Plutarch, I believe—that I came to understand that the thoughtlessness of youth does not change with time, only with maturity. The wise man wrote that when young boys cast stones at a turtle, it may be sport to the youngsters—but the turtle is dying in earnest. Gophers, too.

Pests were another matter. Where I grew up, no one much minded when you shot into a tree alive with screeching starlings or blackbirds, their droppings raining onto neat neighborhood sidewalks and vehicles and lawns. I know of more than one small town that briefly waived the ordinance against discharging firearms within the city limits in order to discourage roosting hordes of migrating birds.

And even today, farmers wage their continuing war with the woodchucks and deer and other hungry crop raiders that take money from their pockets and feed from the rumina of their dairy or beef stock. The deaths of some birds and animals can be eternally justified—or rationalized. As for others, I truly wonder.

I have never been comfortable shooting prairie dogs with scoped, sandbagged varmint rifles, for example. Yet I confess to having spent time sprawled prone under a cloudless east Montana sky, eyeing a distant target and easing off rounds that kicked up plumed geysers in the prairie dust or exploded dumb rodents into lifeless masses of bloodstained fur and exposed entrails. Their mounded burrows, I suppose, do pose something of a threat to careless range stock. They do eat meager prairie grasses, too. Disease is possible, I'm told. And a lot of ranchers I know hold a deep and abiding dislike for them, actively seeking their eradication with indiscriminate poisons and selective rifle shots alike. But for the most part, prairie dogs seem to live harmless, peaceful lives and die violent deaths in out-of-the-way places where kestrel and coyote, rattler and badger and black-footed ferret kill in order to live, as it always has been, as it always will be—until some meddlesome human changes the course of natural events. Again.

Selective shooting, I'm convinced, following written or un-written rules, is something else. Moving close—like some bellying, unseen, tail-twitching cat, its full attention locked on a would-be meal, inching closer step by silent step, muscles tensed, ready to strike—gives any prey a chance and any thinking predator a deep satisfaction that is mostly unfound in dispensing long-distance death.

I once saw a distant groundhog waddling across a field of newly sprouting corn, angling toward a nearby woodlot. It was springtime warm as I rested my .22 on a fence post, aligned the iron sights—holding high because of the range—and squeezed off a single long-rifle round. To my surprise, dust blossomed amid the five-inch green shoots at almost the exact spot where the ground-hog had paused. Jerking as if hit, the brown form moved in a small circle and paused again. I quickly shot several more rounds, ob-scuring the target amid geysers of fine dust. And when the echoes faded, even as the earthy scrim settled to reveal the still form of the groundhog, I scarcely believed what I'd done.

The hundred-and-four paces from fence post to dead ground-hog—stepped off twice to verify the accuracy of my count—did briefly evoke a swelling of prideful accomplishment. But I knew I'd been more lucky than good. And I never attempted such a shot again with an open-sighted .22. Some shots, like some vivid slices of other living experiences, are forever burned into your memo-ries, never meant to be repeated or recaptured.

Like the time I slipped within easy bow range of a groundhog busy feeding beneath a four-strand barbed wire fence. A wind stirred the deep grass and clumps of foxtail as the big rodent sud-denly stood, ursine fashion, facing me at a dozen yards. I knew my arrow had flown true, hitting, passing through, and then skipping thirty or forty yards across the pasture beyond the fence. Yet the groundhog never seemed to move. Amid the screen of waving grass, he still merely stood there—a ghost groundhog, perhaps—facing a very confused young bowhunter who dumbly fumbled for a second shaft.

I didn't shoot again. Or need to. My first shot had centered in the animal's chest. The arrow's honed head had sliced away one poised forepaw upon entering and severed the spine while exiting. The arrow's impact had pushed the groundhog against the fence, where a single barb on the lowest strand caught in the scruff of his neck hair and left him hanging, yet appearing to still stand. But for a brief time I faced a ghost groundhog I can never forget, haunted by the sight and the realization that this is not a game. Nor is it sport for some of the participants.

Back to the business at hand. I point out a gopher scolding us from atop his earthen mound, encouraging a shot. Your arrow flies low, but no matter. All across the horse pasture there is scurrying, whistling chirps. We retrieve your arrow and wander on through the weighty spring sunshine. Perspiration glistens on bared forearms, wetting the straps of your armguard.

These may well be ghost gophers, too. How else can you explain the arrows that pass through tiny targets without apparent effect? You release and watch the blur of Technicolor fletching and fluorescent nock speed toward that exact spot you've picked. Yet in the instant before inevitable impact, with the poised ground squirrel incapable of reacting, there is a blending of shaft and target and freshly dug earth. And although you *see* your arrow strike furred flesh, there it is, quivering briefly, in the mound of dirt beyond the burrow's mouth. And the ghost gopher is gone!

You ask about my horse pasture rules again. But there are no exceptions to my twenty-five-yard restriction. At closer range the ghost gophers become all too real. They can be pinned with routine regularity, dying at the entrances to their dens in bloody testimony to the triumph of technology.

Somewhere in the pines a raven croaks agreement. Overhead a magpie rises and dips, rises and dips like a kid's black-and-white kite wavering on unseen twine. We move on. There are far more misses than hits. But there is satisfaction from a well-made shot and quick, clean kill. When dispensing death is a goal, dignity must be maintained. Otherwise the death becomes meaningless. A waste.

The morning grows hotter. Our shirts cling wetly; sweat

stings our squinting eyes. The gophers go underground at last and we walk up into the pine shadows to sit, talk, and wait for nothing in particular. Later today we'll swap your bow for a pair of fly rods, walk down the bluff to the Flathead, and offer dry flies to the cutts and rainbows and whitefish waiting there in the riffles and quiet pools along the edge of rushing, green water with opalescent spray mist rising over wet river rocks.

"What are the rich folks doing?" you wonder aloud. We both smile with the familiar knowing and understanding of friends passing time together. I do not answer because no answer is called for. But I fervently hope that all such times, such moments and their lessons, will never cease to satisfy—and teach—both of us. We'd all be far poorer if the little things of life didn't fire our imaginations, give us new insights, and fuel magic times together that are easy to experience but so difficult to explain.

The Piranha of Pierre

ONE FALL I journeyed to South Dakota for the annual Governor's Hunt held on the undulating prairies that rise from the Missouri's riverbanks near Pierre. And though I'd heard all about the pheasants—and while packing, even daydreamed of cackling roosters climbing into a teal blue sky—no one had told me about the piranha. There are some things you have to discover for yourself.

This invitational hunt is a big event for a lot of people, I suppose. After all, it gives you a chance for a long weekend away from work pressures, family problems, and other real-world concerns. Once there you can hobnob with state bigwigs and captains of industrial concerns being wooed to relocate or expand their companies on South Dakota soil. And if you can endure the Dakota-is-a-great-place commercials, along with the mandatory evening socializing, you can have a great time. I went mostly out of curiosity—and to check out the hunting.

Most of us there chose to go after ringnecks, although there were goose blinds waiting in grain fields at various hunt clubs near reservoirs along the meandering Missouri. And fat, migrating mallards, we were told, could be decoyed off rocky points. A few hardy souls even packed fishing gear with their scatterguns, hoping for a chance to sample the waiting waters of Lake Oahe for walleyes, salmon, and late-season pike. They talked of trying Antelope Creek–Farm Island and testing the tailwaters near the dam. Or Sharpe, maybe Joe Creek to West Bend, although summer is likely better. Or even driving over to Francis Case. Or wherever. It's the doing, the being there, that really matters.

But like I said, I went to sample the South Dakota pheasant shooting I'd heard and read about since I was as tall as the Browning I packed along with my brush pants, flannel shirt, blaze-orange shooting vest and cap, and the most comfortable walking boots I owned.

What I found didn't disappoint. The pheasants have never bounced back from their down years, but Dakota still has millions of the gaudy birds. That's plenty for me. Plenty, in truth, for anybody.

Growing up in southern Illinois doesn't give a boy with a shotgun much opportunity to go after pheasants. Sure, I can remember the time back in the fifties when someone got the idea to transplant ringnecks in Wabash County. And I seem to recall that some local conservation club worked hand in glove with the fish-and-game boys to introduce pheasants to the wild. But this worked out like a lot of things arranged by well-meaning folks who tamper with nature. After a time, everybody gave up on the idea.

I don't know for sure, but I imagine those pen-raised pheasants sure fed a lot of foxes. At least that's what happened on and around Melba and Raymond's farm near Cowling. For a time afterward we'd jump an occasional rooster or hen while working the quail and rabbit patches there, but pretty soon the long-tailed birds simply vanished. Gone. Like the passenger pigeon. And if you wanted to shoot Illinois pheasants, as before you had two choices: head north up Highway 1 or visit a put-and-take preserve.

Preserve pheasants aren't much of a challenge, really. But though I realize that now, I didn't know it then and admit spending more than one day on pay-as-you-go properties where the bird limit is determined only by the number of dollars in your billfold. It's pheasant shooting, not pheasant hunting. If you don't mind that — or don't know the difference — it's okay, I guess.

What happens, I found out later, is that the birds are taken from their pens just before you head out with the dogs and their handler. They're carried into the fields in cages, removed, and spun around. Spinning dizzies them, so when they're placed in the weeds for the dogs to find later, they'll likely still be there. Even if they do recover and run, they usually won't go far. Probably it's because they've never been free before and don't know how to act. They certainly don't act like wild birds. But I didn't have any basis for comparison back then. For all I knew, *all* pheasants held tight.

I was probably seventeen or so before I shot my first wild pheasant. My oldest sister, Margie, and her husband ran a motel near Rochelle in those days. They'd sold their farm and moved to Ogle County, where they played innkeepers for tourists heading up to Wisconsin. Sonny, my nine-toed nephew, told me about the pheasants he heard crowing in the fields and saw feeding along the roads. So I arranged a visit just before the season opened, heading north with my cased Remington in the trunk.

Just after sunup, Sonny and I worked a weedy ditch in back

of the motel. We had King along but he wasn't much help, even though he probably believed he was a bird dog, not a beagle, on that sunny fall day. While he nosed along, these pheasants mostly sprinted ahead of us, flushing wild, rocketing away to glide on locked wings into the Del Monte asparagus field across the highway. But it was opening day and there were a lot of birds around. Even two teenagers and a beagle could soon limit out on uncautious stragglers. Within the hour we were on our way back to motel headquarters with Sunday's dinner—four rainbow-hued, honest-to-God wild ringnecks—carried proudly in the bulging game pockets of our hunting jackets.

I remembered that hunt when I watched the first South Dakota pheasants flush wildly ahead of an advancing line of drivers and come jetting our way. I thought this must have been how it would have looked if somebody had been standing in the asparagus field when King, Sonny, and I worked that weed-choked ditch nearly thirty years ago. And then the first birds were on us and time for reminiscing was past.

I've had easier wing shooting. Of course, I'd never been a stander before with flushed wild birds passing full-out overhead. And even though the cornfield drivers and the other standers tried to help, shouting "Rooster!" or "Hen!" as the pheasants became airborne in the distance or closed in enough to make identification possible, it was tough. You had, at best, only a few seconds to decide whether the feathered missile was legal and, if so, what to do about it.

Three of us were standing along an earthen dam around a pothole below a picked cornfield. Some of the birds set their wings and coasted into the cattails surrounding the pond in front of us. Others had distant places on their minds, and these were the ones that attracted our full attention.

I missed a rocketing rooster with the modified barrel but somehow took him going away with the full. He folded neatly, did a half turn in midair, and slanted into the weeds below the embankment. I marked the spot, turning confidently back to the business at hand in time to miss another rooster crossing high to my right. I've had easier pass shooting.

It took our ten-man team maybe three hours to fill our daily limit of thirty birds. We probably drove six or eight fields all told, keeping careful count of the roosters we downed and piled in the back of two pickups. And when the shooting finally stopped and we headed back to the host rancher's house for lunch, we took justifiable pride in the fact that no hens had been accidentally shot and that every rooster we'd hit had been found.

Counting shells, I discovered I'd shot fourteen times to account for two clean kills. But, I rationalized, there were three times when I'd been driving and roosters rose suddenly ahead of us and two—sometimes three—shotguns swung and fired together as one in that *whump-whump-whump* so familiar to groups of drivers in good pheasant cover. Who killed those birds was anyone's guess. But, standing there and reloading as dogs made the retrieve, we each smugly knew ours had been the shot that mattered. Only modesty kept us from saying so.

Regardless, at best I'd managed only one bird for every three shots. Pheasants have a way of humbling a lot of wing shooters, and I was in some pretty good company.

Once I killed a flying northern Indiana pheasant with a flu-flu hunting arrow. It was the first rooster I'd ever shot at with my bow. When the pointer locked in on a suspicious clump of weeds, I simply nocked the arrow and walked past the quivering dog. The rooster came up cackling, flying straight ahead, offering one of those relatively easy going-away shots all pheasant shooters prefer. And though I didn't remember drawing and releasing, suddenly my arrow was in the bird, the outsized spiral fletching just under the tail feathers, and that rooster was drunk-wobbling down in a losing fight with gravity. While I won't mention how many of my arrows have missed flying pheasants, I do know I'll never forget that one good shot.

I'll never forget walking those South Dakota fields either. Not because this Governor's Hunt was anything special to me. But because even in a crowd of orange-capped bird hunters, I could be alone with my thoughts, content in the knowledge that other hunters once walked these same hills long before pheasants came to North America. These first known hunters were Arikara and Mandan—Dakota Sioux. Later, Lewis and Clark's men passed this way. And later still, Custer and his troopers. All saw the same rolling lands, felt the same eternal wind. All, like me, were men heeding some distant calling that I know but can't explain. This, too, is good company to be in.

Riding back to town in a sudden late October snow squall, past the exact spot in Fort Pierre where in 1743 Louis and François La Vérendrye stood and claimed these lands for France, I reflected on all those who had passed here before. What would they think of it today — of the houses and buildings; of the paved-over wagon trails and their flow of noisy, rushing vehicles; of the steel and concrete bridge spanning waters where sweating men once poled their way north and later the smoke-belching steamboats churned? It was something to ponder.

So was Noah, the piranha swimming in endless circles in a lighted aquarium in the motel restaurant. Huge, dark, unblinking, he moved silently through the gray water like the hand of death, while beyond the glass people ate and talked and tried not to stare. But between bites and snatches of conversation, we felt our eyes drawn back to this unexpected predator slowly finning, turning, lazily measuring his space in the same way as does a pacing lion across a gaping zoo moat. The piranha's mouth, held in its frozen pout, hid those terrible teeth. But we knew they were there.

I wondered if the goldfish knew of those teeth. Half a dozen of the sacrificial fish shared the piranha's tank, swimming together, just ahead of circling death. The passive aquarium giant's unhurried movements were reassuring, almost hypnotic, until — with a surprising quickness that belied his bulk — the piranha surged ahead, inhaled, and six goldfish became five. Seconds later scales and a milky fluid escaped the giant's gills and settled slowly to the gravel below, as the survivors and the piranha resumed their circling death dance.

A plastic sign beside the tank provided facts about the fish, a black pacu piranha born in the Amazon in 1969. Noah had been only three inches long when he arrived in Pierre after spending several years in a Sioux City inn. He had quadrupled in size since then. At the tables, fascinated diners guessed his weight, wondering aloud how often a goldfish disappeared, staring despite themselves.

Meanwhile, just across the river in downtown Fort Pierre, at a game-processing plant conveniently located behind a taxidermy studio, stiffening pheasants in bulging cardboard boxes awaited their turns before the whirring picking machines and clacking knives. And in the motel there was a bustle of preparatory activity for the banquet that would cap another successful Governor's Hunt weekend.

Walking the carpeted corridors of that crowded prairieland motel, I came to the realization that not all of the piranhas in Pierre swim behind glass. Nor are goldfish their only prey. But there are some things you must discover for yourself.

NINETEEN

A Day in Hell's Canyon

IT IS DAYBREAK in Hell's Canyon, springtime cool, and breath ghosts float about our faces as we collect our fishing gear, move down from the tents to the water's edge, and clamber aboard the two waiting boats for the ride upriver. The Snake sweeps past, murmuring.

Earlier, standing motionless on the rocky shore, I watched the dark water roll by and felt the chill of a faint breeze against my face and beard. The moving wind and water gave the land itself a sense of motion. Now, feeling the actual pitch and roll of the deck beneath my boots, I shiver with the anticipation of this day's movement toward adventure, discovery.

The jet boats surge to life and move easily out into the strong current. We huddle out of the wind, watching Oregon slip past on our right, Idaho on the left. A lone white-cheeked Canada goose watches us pass. I can see its head swivel, beak opening and closing, and in my mind I hear the *har-onk* though my ears hear only the deep roar of powerful engines.

We fish the deep pools for sturgeon, leapfrogging our way upriver as the rising sun spills over rolling, green hills and warms the canyon's rocks and air. Chukars call from the high slopes. Deer and an occasional band of elk look up from their browsing to watch us pass. We spin cast for trout and smallmouth bass while keeping an eye on the heavy sturgeon lines. The gamefish we catch are hacked into wedges and impaled on outsize hooks. Our guide has promised they make the best bait for the prehistoric bottom feeders we seek.

I've come here with friends, out of inner need, to confront a primitive link with my past. I've also come to personally examine the remnants of a once-wild river, tamed forever by modern man for his convenience and seasonal amusement. I seek evidence of a wildness I know must remain here. Somewhere.

The wild Snake, twisting south and west out of the shadows of the Tetons on its thousand-mile serpentine journey toward the Columbia, swells with meltwater, and spreads into Lewis and Jackson lakes before cascading northwest to tumble into steep canyons of conglomerate rock.

Arcing suddenly south across lava plateaus, it forms steplike cataracts to emerge from the shadows tamed by dams, canalled, bleeding life into semiarid lands where sheep and cattle and grains exist only because of the once-wild waters. Then west and north once more, into deep, black lava canyons, washing against waiting concrete dams and freed again, the river continues beyond to where we ride the current in laddered pools with sequined riffles, watching the slant of lines for signs of life beneath rushing green waters flecked with swirling foam.

And then, sometime after midday, I feel the fish and set the hook. Past and present merge, linked in time and space. My heart begins to pound as I crank the heavy reel. But he will have none of it. He simply turns into the current and rides it down into another pool as I watch the braided line feeding from its spool, humming as it goes.

I somehow work him back upriver, dipping the rod tip and cranking on the downsweep, raising the rod, straining, then simply waiting, resting. Repeating it again. But it is as if I have hooked some living, unseen log. He is dead weight for a time, then suddenly alive, pulling away. There are times I try to move him and I cannot. The tangent of the taut line in the rushing water is unmoving, unmovable. And I am awed by his strength, humbled by my own frailty. We struggle on.

This is far different fishing than I am used to. In the Flathead, below my bluff, I can step into the river shallows and feel the cold current sucking against my legs, the slippery gravel sliding beneath the soles of my waders. I unhook a dry fly—a Royal Wulff this time, with its touch of red—from the cork handle, stripping line from the reel with my left hand, and cast it upstream into the little waves of the current. I strip more line as the small fly floats past and finally circles shoreward, bobbing in the little waves.

My eyes do not leave the fly. The trout simply suck it under at times. Or they take it in with a rolling rush. Either way, you have to be ready to lift the rod tip before they taste the steel or the Squip and spit out the fly before you can react. And even watching, fully alert, you still miss more sets than you think you should. But there are those magic times when you see or sense the strike and feel the tug as your graphite rod bows with the pull and comes alive in your hand.

The thing I like most about battling a wild trout is the visual and visceral excitement of the fight. Trout are sleek, beautiful, rainbow-mottled fish whose sides flash in the sun as you work them to the waiting net. They are genteel, generating an electrical spark of satisfaction, win or lose, and giving contentment to mind and gut alike.

Sturgeon, I am coming to discover, are different. Ugly, brutish, they are most often skulking brawlers who seek to steal your bait unseen — not with the grab of trout but with the determined pull of salmon — and when caught at it, they fight you with a strength and resentment that can make you question your commitment to the struggle. And your own courage. It is an uneasy, disturbing confrontation.

They know intimidation, too. Earlier in the day a huge fish Randy hooked rose and broke water downstream, half emerging like a lazy bass or tarpon, to shake its head and fall back with a heavy splash as if someone had dropped a slate gray boulder into the pool.

"A seven-footer," someone said.

"Eight," our guide said.

And none of us doubted it even though the fish threw the hook and we could never know for sure.

My fish is no acrobat. He stays deep and uses the current each time I try to work him near the boat. My hands and arms ache. A photo someone later sends me shows pain in my face, too. At the moment I only want it to end soon, one way or the other.

It is a long half hour or more before I finally see him, turning tiredly in the current off the boat's stern. There in the water, just below the surface, he reminds me of one of the sharks someone always managed to hook over the snapper banks in the Gulf off Galveston. None was ever boated, I remember, and I wonder if this struggle will end in the same way.

I tell myself I don't really care. But I do. This has become personal. And I return to the business at hand.

The guide works his boat to the Oregon shore. And with the end finally in sight, I find renewed strength in numbed arms, hands, and fingers. I drop the rod's tip and crank the reel, pulling the weary sturgeon — trailing the boat now like some sodden, partially submerged log — ever closer, until he is in the shallows. I step from the boat onto the rocks. Randy drops into the knee-deep water and slips a rope over his tail, snugging the loop tight. It is over.

Kneeling beside the ganoid fish, a six-footer that our guide guesses might weigh 125 to 130 pounds, I study the living fossil by wetting my hand and running my fingers over its pointed snout and the rows of bony plates along its back.

I read somewhere that a large female is capable of laying three million eggs. And though the thought of that much cavier stuns me, I have no reason now to doubt. I have also heard that these fish age much like humans, maturing in their late teens and early twenties. If that is true, a fish this size could be my age, perhaps older.

We turn the tired fish onto its side there in the shallows so that I can remove the hook from its protruding, obscene mouth ringed by the four sensory barbels that led it to the bait and ultimately to me.

Without the containment of the dams, this sturgeon and others of its Acipenseridae kind would migrate to the sea, returning to the rivers only to spawn. But even this river giant would be small in comparison with some of the great fishes of the open seas. And there it surely would be preyed upon by predators — including ingenious man — seeking its rich, red flesh for food, its air bladder for isinglass. Here, at least, remote and mostly unknown, it can exist in relative peace and safety, living out its years without seeking freedom — or paying its price.

Can true freedom, I wonder, ever be missed if existence of that freedom has never been known? Animal instinct aside, I'm convinced that fishes and fowls and beasts, without human capacity for rational thought, cannot yearn for what they do not know; they simply experience. Only some of us thoughtful creatures curiously — perhaps enviously — seek answers and freedoms in wildness; others simply exist, like the sturgeon, unaware of what lies beyond the canyon walls.

Given the choice, I would come to this place afoot, alone, working my way upriver over the upthrust rocks without any guide but the sun and stars. That would be a search of another kind, without benefit of jet boat and leased knowledge, a search for discovery of sturgeon and self. That way I could offer myself, unconditionally, accepting as truth all I touch and all that touches me. But that dream is censored by the conspiracy of time, habit, and convenience. I am not alone.

So I stand beside friends and fish, slipping the noose from around the sturgeon's tail, gently righting him, guiding him from the shallows toward deeper water. He is still sluggish, resting there on the gravel, his ridged back above the river's surface. I stroke its smooth coolness a final time. Then, with a sweep of his tail, he moves away and quickly disappears into the fast, dark water.

I do not fish any more that day. I watch the others and help with the landings. But it is different for me now. Mostly I just recall what has happened and work at understanding why. It is not an easy task.

Driving back to Boise late in the cool night, my spent friends quiet or dozing beside me, I continue to relive the day in Hell's Canyon, and I think of the river and the fish. Somewhere between Cascade and Smiths Ferry I decide that my search for wildness was successful. This day has helped me understand that to find wildness you do not have to explore fast waters or land a fossil fish; but if wildness exists in the mind, you can find it anywhere there is space to seek the source of the restlessness in your soul. It is not an especially memorable discovery, merely a satisfying one.

I also realize that, indeed, what once was can never be again. Accept that, I have come to believe, and it is possible to share the space of raw and rugged valleys, dark canyons with vertical cliff faces rising thousands of feet into cobalt skies, and below — audibly alive — the river draining to the sea, hurrying home. After all, today's wildness is unconditional and complex, ever changing, like time itself.

Tomorrow I will fly home, my thoughts and the soreness lingering in my arms reminding me of a personal, primitive quest even while technology distances me from the source of my discoveries. And tomorrow a great fish will nose along the bottom of a winding canyon river, alternately resting and grubbing for food as it has done for decades, and perhaps it will somehow recall our brief time struggling together before each returned to a familiar and comfortable world.

TWENTY

Thanksgiving Morn

A GOLDENEYE DRAKE swings by the decoys, moving right to left, close overhead. I am clumsy cold, yet my Citori comes up, catches and passes him. I miss clean with the first barrel. But somehow, with more luck than skill, I fold him with the second. He slants limply into the blocks, splashing down into the dark water just beyond our small cattail island. Decoys briefly nod their approval in the spreading ripple rings. It is just past daybreak on Church Slough, Thanksgiving Day, and I already have my first bird of the morning. There is much to be thankful for.

An hour ago we drove through Kalispell's silent streets in the cold dark, the loaded boat trailer rattling behind, the low beams of Todd's truck lights sweeping across frost-encased cars glittering at curbside. We finally headed south on Highway 93, turning east onto the deserted blacktop at Four Corners, then swinging south again along the river, driving slowly, mindful of feeding whitetails frozen in the headlights' glare. Finally there, Dave and I stepped down from the cab's comfort into a brittle cold, switched on flashlights, and guided Todd back down the gravel ramp to the water's edge.

A ten-minute boat ride brought us to the frosty cattail island, but it took nearly twice that time to set out the five dozen mallard and pintail blocks. Dawn was blurring the night sky beyond the cottonwoods across the river by the time we were finished. Ignoring the flocks already winging overhead or landing in our set, we spread camo netting over the grounded johnboat, splashed out through the cattails to a frost-rimed, half-submerged log, fished shells and calls from pockets, loaded our Brownings, and finally settled back to wait for legal shooting time. The lone goldeneye started our morning's shoot.

November is a favorite month of mine. The riverbottom whitetails are in full rut. Overhead you can watch broken skeins of wildfowl thread across sullen, roiling skies. And on certain quiet afternoons, with the autumn sun warm across your shoulders, you can hear the tinkling of dog bells in nearby alder patches. The subsequent whir of wings and the rolling boom of your twelve-gauge are nice but not really necessary. November is a mighty fine month for reflections, too.

Looking out through the cattails across Church Slough, past the inlet to where the Flathead rolls by like liquid slate, I realize that what a hunter hunts is not as important as being there, alone or in the company of friends or family, seeking elusive but essential freedoms. It is a personal quest. An individual test. It also is something those who do not hunt can neither share nor truly understand.

Soon a small flock of mallards sweeps upriver, spots our sprawling set, and passes over us, interested but high, talking to the blocks. Todd talks back to them, greeting the flock with highball runs, keeping his head down, sneaking only sideways peeks. I chatter coaxing feed calls, playing simple background music to Todd's double-reed solo. But they have been decoyed before and will have none of it. The flock turns away and wings upriver again. Somewhere on the peninsula behind us a lazy turkey gobbles in his roost tree. Dave and I exchange knowing looks, and I cannot help but smile at the sheer beauty of the primitive song.

This is a part of what hunting is all about, or should be about: an appreciation of wild things we meet as both predator and prey, the expected and the surprising. But it's really more than that, too. It can be as simple as the mere recognition of another living presence, or a special sharing of a moment in time when you leave your over-and-under across your lap and simply watch the inbound flock land in your decoys. Or as mystical as somehow feeling watchful eyes as you cross a stubble field on the way to an afternoon stand and turning in time to see the statue buck and doe staring from the shadows.

This is the recognition, the acknowledgment of other life, that I mean. This is the sharing I seek.

If you are like me, you have come—or in time almost certainly will come—to understand the occasional need simply to sit and watch rather than act. Sitting and watching may not fill the freezer, but I know for a fact that it can fill the mind and chase the hollow hunger from your soul.

The best hunters I know are observers. Truly. It takes little thought or practiced talent to dump a decoying drake. It is reflex, not reason. I feel that hunting can and should be more. To take without giving something of yourself in return is largely a thoughtless act. Mere appreciation, however brief, often would be enough.

A distant flock of mallards swings above the trees, drifting like dark dust motes in a slant of sudden sunshine, then moves our way. There is no hesitation this time, no need for calls, and they leave three of their kind behind when they flare away and, riding a rising wind, disappear downriver. Dave and Todd wade out to claim their kills. I sit back against the slick log and watch three bounding whitetails splash across an inlet, enter the river current, and swim to the narrow wooded island across from us. Above the naked island cottonwoods a swirl of ducks rises like thin smoke, then settles again beyond the trees. Somewhere behind me, but farther away now, the late-rising gobbler starts swearing again.

I could come back tomorrow, leaving my Citori at home or trading it for my camera, but it would not be the same. And I could likewise sit and watch Todd and Dave fill their limits and mine, but it would not be the same. Or I could sit here, staring skyward until a wavering line appears, then crouch and call until the mallards have had their look-see and swing into the wind, locking their wings and rocking in, and rise to shoot—or not shoot, at my whim. This is what duck hunting, all hunting, is about. The freedom to choose. Choices. Freedom.

Moments later, three lonesome drakes sweep in from our left, slowing to scan our set. We rise out of the cattails as one and score a rare triple—rare for us, anyway—in less time than it takes to tell. And even before the flush of satisfaction in shots well aimed and quick kills cleanly made has a chance to fade, a small flock of mallards swings in from our rear, silhouettes against the lightening eastern sky, intent on joining our decoy set. I again stand without hesitation, swing on what I take to be a drake, and claim this single bird from the middle of the flock. Too late I see it is a hen, and I feel a brief pang of regret as she cartwheels down. True, she is Montana legal, but in these lean times for most waterfowl, I pick my shots as best I can, seeking to claim only drakes. Usually I do just that. And generally I decline to take a legal limit, too, although I could and have. It's just a personal thing with me. Another choice.

The time may come when I will take only a single bird—or

none. That, too, will be my choice. But even then, it is hard to imagine at least one November dawn without having a slough smell around me as I sit crouched in some cattail clump, straining eyes and ears to pick up the approach of the first flight of the new day.

Beside me, just to my left, Dave is shooting. A drake falters with his first shot, fights for altitude, then finally drops when the second string of steel 4s catches up to him. He goes down onto the skim ice of a shallow cove behind our tiny island. At my right shoulder Todd is simply standing, watching. That, this time, is his choice.

Dave and Todd retrieve the ducks and array them across our log, admiring them, smoothing ruffled iridescent feathers. We have enough birds, we know, yet we are reluctant to leave.

At home, as all across this wide land of ours where millions of kitchens already are oven warm, there is a spilling over of the special sounds and smells of Thanksgiving Day. Family and friends are coming, have come, together. It is as it should be. And soon enough we will join them. But for now we are giving appropriate, reverent thanks as hunters, each in his own way, father and son and friend, shoulder to shoulder in a place called Church Slough. To me, at this special time and place, the name fits.

It is not that I am an especially religious man, because, admittedly, I am not. And it is not that I do not believe in God, because, honestly, I do. It is just that some of the best sermons I've heard and seen and remembered are those preached in scintillating autumn air by honed winds carrying the musical cries of wildfowl, rustling the frost-glazed cattails, and giving sudden life to the decoy spread beyond your blind. Such homilies, once heard and heeded, are an answer—if not *the* answer—to finding peace of mind on earth if not in heaven.

At such times I frequently fret over what's happened to most of my life and mull about what I hope to do with the little bit of time that's left. You've thought about it, too, or surely will, given due time and occasion. I'm convinced it's as natural as the need to ponder all of life's mysteries, to ask the eternal *why*.

Finally it is time to go. We unload and case our shotguns, then set about picking up the decoys, filling the net and burlap bags, our wet fingers soon red and numb, complicating even the routine winding of the anchor lines. But soon enough it is done and Todd pulls the cold outboard back to life, pointing the boat into a gentle chop.

Ducks resting on the sandbars near shore watch us pass. We give them wide berth, and they do not fly. A few flocks are still on the wing, trading upriver and down in the near distance, but the morning flight has mostly ended. It is time to rest again.

Among the gray cottonwoods along the moving shoreline a turkey trio of dark Merriams slinks through a tangle of leafless brush. But like the idling ducks, the threesome has nothing to fear from us, earning only our admiration and respect.

Another day it may be different. The choices I spoke of still remain, and the time may come when I — or we — choose to return and seek an end to some wild life. Yet for now the seeing, the being here, is enough.

Soon we are loading the dripping boat onto its trailer at the graveled ramp, snugging the lines, readying it and ourselves for the short drive home. The braked truck idles, waiting, its cold heater blowing cool air into the closed cab. But that same air will have changed to comforting heat by the time we are ready to leave. I am eager to warm stiff fingers over dashboard vents, to feel my face begin to thaw. I fumble with my final loading tasks, thinking too of this day's feast awaiting us at home.

I am nearly finished when I hear the loud and lyrical calls of whistling swans. Three of the big, long-necked birds, two snow-white adults and a darker juvenile, pass slowly overhead, set their wings, turn into the wind, and float down onto the sandy spit opposite the boat ramp. The three of us simply stare, transfixed, watching the swans.

It is just past midmorning on Church Slough, Thanksgiving Day. Todd, Dave, and I indeed have much to be thankful for.

TWENTY-ONE

A Silent Morning

I HAD GOOD INTENTIONS. Really. By rising early, starting the routine springtime yard work I'd been neglecting, yet doing only enough to show Janet I really was serious about keeping my obligatory promise, I knew I'd still have plenty of time to head down the bluff to the Flathead by late morning or early afternoon. It's catch and release in the Montana rivers this time of year, but walking the sandy shoreline and thinking — not serious fishing — was what I really had in mind anyway.

The early May snowstorm we woke to immediately changed my Saturday plans — at least those concerning the yard and garden — and freed me to do as I pleased. Since walking through the falling snow, even without a rod or bow or gun, is a favorite pastime, I knew just how to begin this day. Could I be held accountable if the weather precluded mowing and weeding and hoeing and planting? As I said, I had good intentions. Honest.

Carefully crossing the drifting cattle guard, I raised my coat collar, lowered my hat brim, and plodded down the snowy lane toward the hay barn, hoping the horses were back up in the pines. I knew that if they saw me they'd move down to the barn, whinnying as they trotted through the swirling curtain of downy flakes, expecting to be fed. At this moment I had more pressing business to tend to. Besides, I did not wish to dash any more expectations this morning.

I made it past the barn and into the woods without hearing or seeing the horses. There beneath the trees, out of the wind and under a protective canopy of sagging boughs, I tracked through the fine snow dust and breathed cold, clean air. There are times when a solitary walk seems necessary to clear the week's accumulation of mind clutter. And this was just such a time.

Aimlessly walking and daydreaming, I soon passed the clearing where we'd seen the big tom, two jakes, and two hen Merriams pecking among the green shoots earlier in the week. There I glimpsed a dark shape and paused briefly, staring through the sifting snow. This time it was only a fire-blackened stump, not a wild turkey. I moved on. Soon I found myself on the bluff overlooking the quiet inlet where I've spent time each autumn jumpshooting mallards. On this day the dark water below was empty; beyond the snowy scrim the unseen river whispered past.

Turning away, I followed a freshly tracked deer trail down the bluff. I briefly believed I could smell the faint, musky whitetail scent lingering in the air. But I decided it was the damp-wood smell of spring itself.

Why is it, I've wondered, that a single notion can open a floodgate of questioning after elusive truths? In fact, why is it, I wonder, . . .

. . . some people can manage to live their entire lives without knowing the change of the seasons . . . without discovering the gold in buckskin larch and quaking aspen, seeing the fire maple flaming red in some sunlit clearing . . . without hearing the crush of crisp leaves beneath lugged boot soles . . . without smelling the dusty dead-leaf scent a soft breeze raises in the fall woods . . . without feeling the soft brush of a cobweb against their faces during an early morning walk . . . and without knowing the clinging wetness of pants legs dampened by dew — or by miscalculating the distance to the opposite streambank?

. . . there are magic days when still-hunting beats sitting on stand and waiting — quiet, misty days, especially, or certain cold days that are made for stalking, with a powdery snow underfoot rather than the wet, crystalline flakes that compress into an impossibly noisy squeakiness beneath boot soles?

. . . there are some people who begin conversations by asking about your latest kill — or telling you about theirs — and who really believe it's all that important?

. . . the best hunters and the best anglers consistently fill their freezers regardless of the gear they use, while others experiment endlessly, forever trading or tinkering with their tackle selections yet enjoying only a fraction of the success?

. . . there are newspaper writers who insist on calling poachers "hunters," and for that matter, why do some hunters poach?

. . . you never remember there's a tiny hole in the seat of your waders until you're waist-deep in a trout stream or decoy set . . . and you always somehow manage to lose only one glove?

. . . there are days when you can't miss and days when you can't hit — and there's often a direct correlation to the number of witnesses to your shots?

. . . that hard-hit bucks and bulls usually run downhill and away from roads before going down . . . and that most offers to help dress or drag game come after you've finished that particular chore?

. . . there are some teachers who hate hunting and spread their beliefs in their classrooms . . . some students will have their values influenced by these teachers . . . and neither these teachers nor students know or understand the truth about wildlife?

. . . the most obnoxious sportsmen have the loudest voices . . . insist on wearing T-shirts with offensive slogans . . . get drunk in public . . . never get caught breaking game or fish laws . . . go around bragging about it . . . and are viewed as "typical" hunters by most people they meet?

. . . the haunting sounds of wild geese winging overhead in a starless sky, the eerie bugling of a bull elk in the black timber at daybreak, and the maniacal laughter of loons on a northern lake at sunset can't be heard by more people seeking to experience the essence of wildness?

. . . there are so many shot-riddled highway signs . . . so many gates left open, fences cut, and tire tracks crossing crop fields . . . so many littered campsites, roadsides, and waterways?

. . . the pictures you took of that special trophy didn't turn out . . . or they did but not the way you'd hoped . . . or you shot the last exposure on your last roll of film just before you bagged or boated that once-in-a-lifetime trophy?

. . . there are times you actually believe someone who tells you the bugs aren't bad there that time of year?

. . . there are some people who pay good money to hire a professional guide, then ignore his advice . . . treat guides like servants . . . believe their money is buying them an animal instead of a fair-chase hunt . . . blame everybody but themselves when they go home empty-handed?

. . . you wish, too late, that you'd taken getting into shape — and practicing during the off-season — a lot more seriously?

. . . there are some people who claim to have "built-in compasses" in their heads . . . and a lot of time that could have been spent hunting is spent searching for these same people?

. . . that people who win calling contests often seem to appeal more to human ears than the birds and animals they're imitating . . . and on occasion these birds and animals, in real life, hit sour notes of their own?

. . . there are people who simply cannot understand that the noise pollution of an ATV or snowmobile in the backcountry is viewed by many as no less offensive than breaking wind in a crowded church . . . there are some places that are meant to be walked, not ridden . . . and transistor radios should be outlawed from public campgrounds?

. . . that if you haven't drawn blood fooling with a fishhook or sharpening a broadhead, you haven't done much of either?

. . . there are days when it won't rain simply because you remembered to pack your slicker . . . and vice versa?

. . . that setting up a tent in the dark woods is different from setting up the same tent in the backyard in broad daylight . . . only optimists believe a manufacturer's claim about the number of people their tent will "sleep comfortably" . . . and lightweight backpacking tents are never truly lightweight, especially at the end of a five-mile uphill hike?

. . . that people hunt from tree stands without using safety belts when falls injure and kill more hunters than all gunshots and arrow wounds combined . . . and they actually believe all such accidents happen only to someone else?

. . . that you think paddling a canoe looks easy and say so . . . and you have to discover for yourself that fast water can be downright cold, even in July or August?

. . . there are youngsters who have never gotten sunburned while fishing . . . who have never baited a hook and wiped their fingers on their shirt or pants, impatiently watched a bobber, or felt a pole magically come to life in their hands?

. . . that some people have never had their faces licked by a puppy . . . played fetch or gone for a walk with a dog . . . or later dozed off sitting in a favorite chair with the dog contentedly curled at their feet?

. . . the exact time you pick to stretch, scratch, or stand is the exact time the biggest buck you've ever seen bounds away into the ashy shadows?

. . . there are bowhunters who brag that they "stuck one" and then act bewildered when some listener gets upset . . . there are gun hunters who mention shots they've taken by sound alone and then wonder why people get indignant and why suddenly no one wants to hunt with them . . . there are people who should not be armed with any weapon more dangerous than a flyswatter . . . there are those who, in truth, don't belong in the same woods with you and me?

. . . arguments over religion and politics, stick bows vs. compounds, autoloaders vs. pumps, side-by-sides vs. over-and-unders are always a waste of time and breath?

. . . it's possible to make a checklist and pack a week's worth of clothes and gear, yet still manage to forget something you really need — and not discover the oversight until you're a long way from anywhere?

. . . there's no adequate way to explain the appeal of hunting and fishing to someone who has done neither . . . no way to ever convince an anti that you're right and he's wrong?

. . . that alarm clock in your head works?

. . . that perhaps the greatest gift you can give is setting a good example, teaching — patiently and responsibly — any eager friend or family member how to hunt and fish, to respect wildlife, to obey game laws, and then to later share that knowledge with others?

I suddenly found myself beyond the woods, walking down the snowy two-track that twists through the bayou flats before snaking up the face of the bluff, past the untilled garden and unmowed lawn, leading finally back to the cedar house where Janet would be busy with breakfast or Saturday chores. Already I could imagine the warm kitchen smells, and I quickened my stride.

It was still snowing. But it was a May snow and it would not last. All too soon rain would replace the soft, settling flakes, drumming on the tin roof of the hay barn and streaming off its sloped sides in slender white threads, slapping and matting the sodden grass below. Solitary morning walks in steadily sheeting rain are not all that conducive to thought; give me a silent snowfall anytime.

As I trudged uphill, I knew I would finally stop to throw hay to the horses before returning to the house. And then I would walk back up the lane, past my filled-in tracks, and pause there by the side door, stamping my boots, slapping the snow from my hat and coat before stepping inside. Later, after breakfast, I would sit down and write of the morning walk, of my thoughts, my musings. There would be other spring days spent burning precious time in the garden and yard. This cold day, this early morning had been perfect for a silent walk, alone with my thoughts. This spring day, this snowy morning had been all mine.

TWENTY-TWO

Another Letter Home

DEAR RUDY,

Greetings from Montana! Not long ago a trapper with the U.S. Department of Agriculture's Animal Damage Control Division shot and killed a yearling wolf north of my place. Apparently the wolf, a sixty-pound bitch, had begun to prey on livestock. It was directly blamed for the deaths of two calves in late March, and the same wolf was strongly suspected of killing two other calves.

While shooting the wolf obviously pleased the rancher where the calf killings occurred, it predictably upset area animal rights activists. These folks claimed the animal should have been live-trapped and relocated. As you and I know, capturing wild animals is much more easily proposed than accomplished. But naturally you'll never get any of those vocal animal activists to admit it.

Fact is, the fish-and-wildlife officials had tried without success to capture this wolf when the calf killings were first reported; however, the wary bitch already had a history of being trap shy. I'm told that a year earlier she'd escaped the government traps that captured the rest of her pack on the same ranch after the wolves first began preying on livestock. And when she once again proved too elusive for capture and relocation, her fate was sealed. By early April she was dead, and the antis were doing the howling.

Now, I admit that I don't know much about wolves. You'll recall that even coyotes were rare in Illinois when we were growing up. But I've since read Mech, watched nature films featuring these big canines, and talked to a number of wolf hunters. I do know that wolves are large, intelligent wild dogs that are truly efficient hunters. I also know that wolves, alone or in groups, routinely chase, attack, kill, and eat other animals, including domesticated stock. And, finally, I know that if hungry wolves suddenly showed up in my horse pasture, I'd do whatever I could to encourage the local fish-and-game officials to deter the creatures' attacks on any animals I owned. If that meant killing the wolves to keep my animals safe, so be it.

But the animal rights folks usually don't seem to know very much about wild animals or own stock of their own. This makes it easy for them to criticize killing wolves or whatever for just doing what comes naturally. They also often conveniently forget to acknowledge the fact that man is the most efficient predator of all. And it's easier to get an unsuspecting public emotionally worked up over the death of an uncommon wolf than that of an ordinary calf.

There are exceptions. No one said much on behalf of animal rights when a cougar killed a little boy playing in his rural back-yard south of my place. Even when hunters treed and killed a cougar—later proved by necropsy to be a different cat than the one that killed the youngster—the generally vocal animal do-gooders kept their mouths shut. I guess even they knew the public wouldn't buy the argument that the cougar, like the wolf, was just doing what it naturally did in order to survive—killing things and eating them—and shouldn't be punished. Calves are expendable. Kids are not.

Grown-ups are something else. When wildlife photographers seeking good close-ups of grizzly bears in Yellowstone and Glacier pressured two bruins and got eaten for their trouble, an immediate cry arose not to punish the bears for human stupidity. Innocent kids justify revenge. Mindless adults do not.

That's a fact I recognize from firsthand experience. When my friend Ed Wiseman wrestled, stabbed, and killed the Colorado grizzly that was mauling him, he brought down the wrath of dozens who took time to write. "How dare you kill the bear, the very last survivor of its species in the state? Better that the grizzly kill you than be killed by you. What were you doing on that bear's mountain anyway? What did you do to provoke the bear attack? Why kill the bear? *Why?*" I've read Ed's hate mail. I've also seen his scars—at least the visible ones—and know what choice I would have made. But then I'm a hunter.

I have never killed a grizzly, although I would, without hesitation, in defense of life or property. I thought about this when a brash, troublesome grizzly was trapped less than a dozen miles from my place last spring. And I would eagerly hunt the great bears, too, with bow or rifle if I ever got the chance. I thought about this when a silvertip was sighted near my British Columbia goat camp last fall. And I would not apologize to anyone for taking a grizzly's life. There are far more of the big bruins around—especially in Alaska and Canada—than the animal rights activists would lead us to believe. The same can be said of cougars, too.

I once dispatched a stock-killing cougar, and I do not apologize for that act. When the big cat developed a taste for quarter horses and began making regular raids on a Utah ranch, I followed the government hunter's rangy Plotts to where they had treed the cougar in a ponderosa pine and quickly ended his life with two arrows to his chest. I wrote about it for *Outdoor Life* back in the early 1970s. And I would do it again. But then I'm an outdoor writer . . . and a hunter.

There are some things I would not do again. I would not, for instance, arrow another half-wild bison raised behind a gameproof fence. Shooting that bull was an act I found akin to walking into a pasture and shooting a beef cow. Perhaps it's partly because I botched the job of killing the one-ton animal cleanly: I watched my first arrow strike the broadside bull and barely penetrate his rib cage; then my follow-up arrow hit the stricken bull's ham before, disgusted and eager to end it, I called for a pistol to put the bull down. Whatever the reasons, I admit that some shots hunters make are best never repeated — if ever taken.

But bison do provide a lot of meat, and I readily admit I prefer it to beef. Someday I may kill another. Here in Montana there had been an annual drawing for permits to kill bison that wandered north out of Yellowstone Park. The shooting was halted in '91. Score one for the antis — and common sense. But what you need to realize is that this was killing, not hunting, and that needs to be clearly understood by everyone. The media, the hunter haters, and even the state boys called it a hunt. It wasn't. It was a bison shoot, a controlled slaughter. Brucellosis prevention was the pretense. The way I see it, regulating herd size and generating money for the state coffers was what shooting Montana bison was really all about.

What everyone needs to remember is that killing Yellowstone bison was nothing new. Park rangers shot some four hundred head during the winter of 1943. And during the 1950s and 1960s rangers slaughtered thousands more of the big animals in the Hayden, Pelican, and Lamar valleys. Elk were routinely shot, too. Native Americans ate well on park-killed game that died mostly out of public sight away from television cameras. That's all changed. These latest "hunts" were viewed by millions watching the evening news. You probably saw them yourself back there in Illinois. And predictably, the animal rightists made the most of it. But I see things differently. I'm a hunter. Like you.

You can still hunt — truly hunt — wild, free-ranging bison. But to do so you have to travel north to Alaska or Canada or west to the Henry Mountains of Utah. There the huge, shaggy beasts still live and die in as much freedom as modern man will allow them. Finding, stalking, and shooting one — with gun or bow — is not the greatest challenge on earth. But it beats the annual circus created by the animal rights folks and television reporters each time one of the Yellowstone bison strays and is shot dead.

I get the idea that the so-called animal lovers become all worked up mainly for the benefit of the media. Take away the reporters and their cameras and it's likely that a lot of the protesters would find other ways to spend their time. Of course, I can't say that's true in every instance. After all, I'm a hunter. And at times I'm ashamed of myself and others.

It's the hunters who bring a lot of the problems on themselves. There are days when I swear that if I see one more shot-up road sign, trash-littered campsite, or news story about some hunter-poacher doing something to give all of us a bad name, I am going to hang it up forever. But then I think about a handful of hunters I know who care more about the outdoors and know more about the wild animals they hunt than all of the mouthy animal rights activists put together. And so I decide to stick around a little while longer, fighting the good fight against the antis. And against some of us, too.

The concerned hunters I know truly care; it's not just that they want to keep animals around to be hunted and shot. And since they realize it takes more than emotional rhetoric to preserve and protect our country's wildlife, they spend much of their time and money on what truly means something to them: the animals and a rich hunting heritage. Meanwhile, the antihunting activists raise funds to spend on their hate literature and demonstrations and money-generating schemes, not on the animals they claim they support and seek to save.

I've talked to antihunters. I've read their pleas for money to end the slaughter of helpless animals at the hands of uncaring, egomaniacal butchers with bows, arrows, guns, and other instruments of wildlife torture. I once asked a prominent hunter hater about his literature stating that the black bear had become an endangered species because of hunters with a penchant for finding sows and cubs in their winter dens and killing the hapless, groggy creatures. The black bear, I pointed out, is not an endangered species. Game laws prohibit the slaughter of sows and cubs. How can you print such lies?

I'll never forget his answer. Most people, he said, don't know the facts and don't bother to check. Moreover, emotional appeals like this raise money — and money means strength. We'll beat you hunters, he warned, because we don't have to tell the truth. But you do.

The truth is that this complex issue of animals and their rights is one of high emotions, big-dollar economics, and personal ideals. And because of the complexity involved, there's no easy answer to the problem. I do know that the antihunters are out to bury us, to end all hunting, forever. They just might do it, too.

You and I grew up hunting together. We could sell our bows and shotguns and rifles tomorrow and never go hungry. We can buy everything we need for ourselves and our families — food, clothing, shelter. Everything that once depended on hunting skill and luck is now readily available to anyone with enough paper or plastic to pay for it. But that's really not the point. The point of why we hunt, as you well know, is personal, private, and elemental. So how do you put into words a convincing explanation for someone who has never known the challenges, rewards, and love of a sport involving myriad skills, self-reliance, and a timelessness that links us to our past, our roots? Sadly, I fear, you can't.

So, old friend, I worry that we're all living on borrowed time, viewed as anachronistic relics of an era that was neither kinder nor gentler than what is deemed desirable and acceptable by today's increasingly judgmental standards. About all we can do is to show by good example that not all hunters are blood-crazed barbarians; to provide facts to combat lies told by animal activists and antihunters; to enjoy, with evening close at hand, whatever hours of fading daylight we have left by answering the siren call of woods and fields; and, finally, to offer thanks that we had an opportunity to experience for ourselves that which someday will only be a memory.

I feel no need to apologize for the length or tenor of this letter. You know me well enough to recognize that I am not taking advantage of our friendship—now in its fifth decade—but merely voicing a frustration and concern I know we share.

Give Mary my best. And the next time you and Brandon feel the urge to venture afield, know you are always welcome at my place. There is, for the moment, still time.

TWENTY-THREE

Dealing with Death

MY FIRST SHOT breaks the great buck's back. He collapses heavily among the stunted pines beneath my tree stand, front legs flailing the brittle November grass and patches of old snow where he sprawls.

There is no hurry, I know, but still I rush to end it. Biting at the shooting glove on my right hand, I free cold, wait-numbed fingers and fumble with the stiff haul line, lowering my weapon. Then I unsnap the buckle to my safety belt. Standing and drop-sliding down the white pine's trunk, I can hear only the harsh scraping of my heavy boots, the frantic thrashing of the stricken buck, and the wild pounding of my hunter's heart.

The deer has managed somehow to get his forelegs under him. He is dragging his ruined hindquarters behind him as I approach. The snow creaks tightly with each step, and I see the buck's ears acknowledge my presence although he doesn't turn to look at me. I am thankful for that.

Easily overtaking the struggling deer, I move beside him, hold for the lungs, and shoot him again through the chest. He paws briefly at the frozen ground and tries to rise, twin streams of vapor trailing from the wounds in his side. The buck's final breaths cloud the cold evening air. Feeling more sadness than elation, I step aside and watch him die.

When his struggling ceases, I move to him and grasp a heavy, bone white antler beam, turning his head to rest it in a more natural position. Kneeling, I stroke his rut-swollen neck and thick shoulder, my fingers feeling the fading warmth while smoothing the ruffled pelage. An empty, spreading sorrow tempers any satisfaction. But I know he has had his chance.

I first saw this buck a week or more ago at the onset of rut. He was half-heartedly trailing a slender doe through a light rain that would turn to snow before nightfall. I drew on him twice, perhaps three times in all, but I did not shoot. The range was long, beyond my self-imposed limit for consistent accuracy. So I simply watched admiringly from my stand in the pine, hoping for another chance.

It came two days ago. The great buck, this time in the company of four does, passed beneath me at less than forty yards — but purposefully on the move. Again I drew, swung briefly with him, hesitated, and merely watched him trot out of sight. Afterward, the memory of his wide rack haunted me. Yet I knew I was right again to let him go.

Then, only short minutes ago, I heard a deer walk out of the woodlot to my right. A tall pine, a twin to the one containing my stand, hid the animal until it was nearly under me. A flash of antler shouted "Buck!" seconds before he stepped into the opening beneath me. I recognized him in an instant. At less than twenty yards there was no mistaking this buck. And as he stopped to look back, I shot quickly—hitting high, nearly missing him after all but breaking his back instead—ending it forever for both of us.

It is nearly dark by the time I wrestle the buck into position at the head of a nearby ravine and field dress him. My arms, bathed to the elbows in hot blood, steam in the faint light as I retrieve his heart and liver, slippery warm and heavier than you might think, stand, and begin the uphill hike from the pine grove toward the buttery rectangle of my kitchen window glowing in the near distance.

I haven't taken half a dozen steps when I see them and stop. Two—no, at least three—shadowy does stand silhouetted along the fence line, staring downslope toward me. They are posed as rigidly as concrete deer on a suburban lawn. I can feel their eyes on me. I can sense their acknowledgment of the buck's death. And, standing there, I share their loss. But I know the seed of the great buck is in them. Somehow for me that makes his death more acceptable.

Then, ignoring the silent *Cervidae* trio, I continue purposefully uphill through the cold, late-fall darkness, gripping the deer's cooling organs like some Stone Age savage returning to his cave, wondering if I can ever kill again but knowing full well I can . . . and will.

I first watched an animal die when I was six, maybe seven. And I remember it still.

There was a crisp crack from the .22. I jumped. The steer staggered but retained its footing. Wide-eyed, I stared at the small, black hole centered in the beast's forehead near a swirl of white hair. Then the steer rolled its own widening eyes and took a single step before dropping to its knees in the dusty barnyard.

A man in overalls stepped near and laid his knife's thick blade along the steer's throat beneath the jaw. His hand jerked and blood geysered, darkening the bright steel and staining the thin denim of wash-whitened pants.

"Gotta cut the throat while his heart's still pumping," the farmer explained. "Little rifle don't kill right off. The animal's dead but don't know it. He'll go down for good when he runs outta blood. Meat tastes better if a critter is bled 'fore it dies."

That steer fed us through the fall and into the winter. I ate its flesh eagerly, yet I remembered the pools of dark blood slowly soaking into fine barnyard dust and how a heavy, metallic smell lingered even after the red turned to black.

Catching a chicken for Sunday dinner was part of farm life, too. A straightened wire coat hanger with a hook twisted in one end was a surefire chicken catcher. You simply walked into the pen, into the scattering flock flowing before you like a wave of water kicking in some pond's shallows on a summer day, reached out with the hanger, hooked a fryer by a leg, and drew the squawking bird close enough to grab by the feet. Then you carried it to the stained chopping block, positioned the bird just so, raised the hatchet, let it fall, and released the headless bird for its final, wing-flapping dash. I can still see the severed head lying in the grass by my scuffed boot, its yellow beak opening and closing in soundless protest, its lemony eye dulling, blinking slowly while the bird's mind somehow registers the finality of my actions.

But I also remember the smell of fried chicken above plates heavy with mounds of mashed potatoes hidden beneath rivulets of ladled brown gravy, a warm slab of buttered bread drooping in one hand, a fork clutched in my other.

There on the farm, death was a part of life. Watching, causing death, to me, became as natural as life itself.

I shot my first rabbit when I was eleven. I carried a twelve-gauge pump through a picked soybean field and kicked the cotton-tail from the stubble where a combine had dropped a clump of brown stalks. The cottontail zigzagged away. The shotgun rose and bucked against my shoulder. An unseen scythe of lead pellets cut the rabbit down. We ate the rabbit that same day, spitting occasional shot onto the plate as we chewed the tender, pink meat.

Whirring bobwhite quail—handsome, white-faced cocks and

yellow-cheeked hens—dropped amid puffs of feathers beyond my shotgun's moving barrel. Rusty orange fox squirrels, their mouths and forepaws stained brown from walnut husks, fell among cuttings in the dead leaves beneath nut trees where they had come to feed. Greenheads, jumped from ice-rimmed drainage ditches, cartwheeled into the cattails while my gloved hands jacked spent shells from the chamber and I sucked in sharp winter air with a tang of cordite. And I forever remember slogging from the pit in a muddy field of picked corn, a brace of giant Canadas tolling silently against my back with each step.

No whitetails lived nearby in those days. I was a college student before I hunted and killed my first deer. But I had learned my deadly business well. And those early dealings with animals and death prepared me for the cyclical business of life. Few people today are similarly blessed.

How can any man or woman, city born and bred, expect to know firsthand—to *understand*—that killing is a daily part of life for all of us? They know, of course. But a lack of thoughtful interest, even outright denial, is easier without any personal involvement. Such people are safely distanced from the death of the meat they eat, the leather they wear. Unlike me, they have never watched a steer or chicken die. Unlike us, they have never killed for themselves. There is no blood on their soft, white hands.

They pay someone else to do their killing. The veal cutlet on the platter is simply meat, not a brown-eyed, milk-fed, living and breathing calf born and raised for the sole purpose of slaughter somewhere out of sight behind concrete-block walls. There is no blood, urine, and fecal matter mingling on the polished aisles of grocery stores. There are no steaming piles of intestines, no sounds of hide being ripped away from muscle, no odor of death in the conditioned air. No, the veal they eat appears miraculously among other choice cuts of meat, wrapped in sanitary cellophane, weighed and priced by the pound, waiting in stainless-steel coolers behind whispering glass doors. Not dead animals. Meat.

And today's fried chicken comes similarly prepackaged or in candy-striped cardboard boxes. There are no headless bodies doing their death dances. No hands reaching into the warm abdominal cavity, fingers pulling entrails and organs free. No scalding water loosening feathers while filling the air with that cloying wet-chicken smell. Not dead birds. Meat.

Again, how can anyone who hasn't seen and touched death know or understand? I know, in fact, that they cannot. And I realize that each successive sheltered generation in turn widens the growing chasm between man and the land. Between those of us who kill and those who are mere consumers. Users.

Righteous modern man says, "Let us call ourselves 'civilized' and pick and choose which animals live and which die and by what means. Let us pay others to kill the animals we need for food and clothing; however, let us look with disdain upon those who still kill for themselves as did their ancestors and their ancestors' ancestors."

Sadly, I note, we live in an increasingly hypocritical world. If the emotional issue is one of life itself, I ask, does not the calf waiting in the feedlot surely value its existence as much as the deer standing in the forest shadows? Yet what choice or chance does the fatted calf have when human wisdom determines it should die? And how many calves ever escape their prescribed fate? Compare the calf with a fawn, born free yet fated by nature to almost certainly die a violent death. Such is the way of wild things. So what is it, I muse, that somehow makes veal acceptable table fare while venison is not? If it is not a matter of life, it surely must be the means of death.

Walt Disney lied to all of us. Brutal death is a daily part of life in wild places. Bambi is an anthropomorphic children's story. Deer do communicate, but they do not talk to one another in human voices. Any animal sound it is possible to name or imitate—the snort, howl, grunt, bleat, bark, roar, cough, or mew—is a poor substitute for human speech, just as the stamping of a hoof, the flick of an ear or tail, and the flashing of erectile rump hair are inadequate substitutes for human gesturing or posturing.

And though wild animals recognize death, they neither anticipate its coming nor cognitively reason ways to avoid it. Maternal instruction, innate instinct, and firsthand experience based on trial and error may be excellent tools of survival; however, too many predators feed daily on the weak and unwary and too many roadways are dotted with the unrecognizable pulp of careless wildlife to credit wild things with self-preserving logic or thought.

Few wild animals die of old age. And their fate, their early death, is not cruel; it is simply the way of the wild. While some may call Mother Nature harsh, uncaring, savage, merciless, implacable, unrelenting — and worse — she defies all these humanistic accusations. Her world was around long before modern man, with his troubled conscience, stepped in. Quite likely it will be around after the last human animal joins the dodo and the dinosaur in the oblivion of extinction.

Despite our ever-changing, ever-indignant world with its growing ignorance of and indifference to the ways of the wild, I remain a predator, pitying those who revel in artificiality and synthetic success while regarding me and my kind as relics of a time and place no longer valued or understood. I stalk a real world of dark wood and tall grass stirred by a restless wind blowing across sunlit water and beneath star-strewn sky. And on those occasions when I choose to kill, to claim some small part of nature's bounty for my own, I do so by choice, quickly, with the learned efficiency of a skilled hunter. Further, in my heart and mind, I *know* the truth and make no apology for my actions or my place in time.

Others around me may opt to eat only plants, nuts, and fruits. Still others may employ faceless strangers to procure their meats, their leathers, their feathers, and all those niceties and necessities of life. Such is their right, of course, and I wish them well. All I ask in return is that no one begrudge me — and all of us who may answer the primordial stirrings within our hunters' souls — my right to do some of these things for myself.

TWENTY-FOUR

Born Too Late?

THERE ARE DAYS when I grow weary of man's pollution, of so-called progress, and of the endless press of a swelling population. At such times I like to picture myself astride a leggy paint, a sleepy pack mule in tow, reining in on a shadowy bluff above the rushing, green waters of some snow-fed mountain river. Overhead an osprey, a struggling trout grasped firmly in its talons, banks beyond the dark pines, turning into the same wind that stirs my flowing beard and dangling hair.

I'm wearing a low-crowned wool hat with two eagle feathers jutting from its beaded band. My fringed buckskin shirt is brain-tanned and smoked dark to turn rain and dew. My soft trousers, slick with buffalo grease, are covered crotch to moccasins with leather leggings. The leather belt girding my middle holds a sheathed Green River knife and a tomahawk thonged in place on my right hip. A backup percussion pistol thrust into the waistband sash is an uncomfortable but reassuring weight against my stomach. A percussion cap holder, crafted by hand from the end of a bison horn, hangs on a short thong from the shoulder strap supporting my powder horn.

The heavy .53 caliber rifle resting across my saddle is a shooter's dream. Crafted in Saint Louie by the brothers Jacob and Samuel Hawken, she shoots center and packs wallop enough to drop a fat buffalo cow at three hundred paces, stop a riled silvertip's charge, and seriously dissuade a brave Crow or Blackfoot warrior from counting coup or lifting hair.

Trail weary, I shift in the creaking saddle and breathe deeply, filling my lungs with sharp mountain air. Tangy scents of pine bough and horse sweat tickle my nose as my chest swells with each long, satisfying drink of sweet high-country air. But a nagging tiredness and grumbling stomach remind me I haven't eaten since first light, and then only a blackened slice of stringy buffalo jerky I'd pulled from my parfleche and chewed as I saddled up for the day's ride.

A gaggle of low-flying Canada geese move upriver, talking among themselves. I watch them out of sight and listen to their haunting cries linger briefly, then dissolve. As if on cue my stomach rumbles again with the thought of dark, juicy goose breast cooking on a spit over dancing flames.

As I turn, I see my pony's ears perk up. He is staring down the bluff at a brushy island of willows and cottonwoods. Something is moving in the shadows. Slowly, silently, a forkhorn buck materializes and moves cautiously into the open, its head erect, sensitive nostrils sorting scents carried on the evening breeze.

Easing my heavy Hawken from its buckskin sheath, I raise the rifle and drop the buck where he stands. Moments later, taking time only to reload and tether pony and pack mule, I kneel, knife in hand, over the warm body of the sleek deer. Soon, strips of dripping backstrap and liver hang suspended on sharpened green sticks beside a crackling driftwood fire easily started with my flint and steel. I crouch watching, licking my lips as the tempting aroma of cooking venison rises over flickering yellow-blue flames.

Finally, unable to wait a second longer, I squat close and grab a stick of sizzling meat. Carving off a generous slice of half-cooked backstrap, I fill my mouth and grunt contentedly as I gingerly chew the hot venison. I eat quickly and greedily with oily juices shining on fingers and lips and chin whiskers. Only after I have gorged myself do I wipe my greasy mouth, hands, and knife blade on sleeves and leggings, belch loudly, and sit back on my heels to watch the fire burn down while shadows close in and the river murmurs beyond the willows.

This is a good place, I know. A man could be alone here, but never lonely. There's an ideal cabin site on the high bluff, with abundant wood and water. There's belly-deep grass for the stock. And the high mountains rising like stockade walls on each side of this long valley could resist the advancing attacks of howling winter storms, holding back the deepest snows. The surrounding valley is alive with deer and elk, moose and bears; the craggy cliffs to the north and east hold bands of surefooted mountain sheep and goats. Tawny mountain cats skulk in the shadows. Grouse drum and call in the distance. Bobcats, foxes, coyotes, and wolves ghost through the brush. Ospreys and eagles glide above the treetops, soaring in the updraft of rising thermals. Fish dart like silver shadows in sparkling, icy river waters, dimpling certain calm coves with telltale rings where they rise to feed. Wedges of wildfowl trade overhead, and thick-furred beavers swim in the shallows of stair-step pools behind log-and-earth dams. Yes, a man with a good rifle, a double-barreled smoothbore, ample powder and shot, and a dozen Newhouse traps need never be hungry or cold here.

But that would come later. Now, game trails beckon beyond the next ridge line. Other hanging valleys await me. I have more rushing streams to ford, more granite mountains and grassy plains to cross. I still hanker to seek out other hidden wild places no white man has ever seen or explored, far from the farms and settlements and outposts at my back. These truly are shining times, by God, and I need only my wits, skill, and a good pony between my knees to own the world.

One day, if my luck holds and the wild critters don't end up scattering my bones across some unknown canyon or coulee, I just might point my pony back toward this special place on a high wooded bluff above the cold river dividing this long valley. It is truly a place a man like me could call home. And mean it. It is a place a man like me senses he'll see again, in this life or the next, because to my way of thinking heaven itself couldn't be any prettier. And once I grow weary drinking the heady wine of freedom, I know I could be content in my final days settling down and sipping the mellow, aged wine of my own destiny.

It is July warm the next time I walk the same shaded bluff I have seen a million times in my mind's eye. This day Janet and I are dressed in cotton and denim; metal, fiberglass, and chrome have replaced horseflesh and pack mule. Now we stand together looking down on the same transparent, green waters I've imagined rushing past wooded islands. Yet this is real. In the near distance snow-crowned peaks rise into an impossibly blue sky, and far across the valley shimmering shadow mountains float against the horizon. A soft breeze stirs the cottonwood leaves and pine needles around us. The nearby cedar house and outbuildings overlook the valley, where other homes now stand. There's also a soft, distance-muted sound of highway traffic, and far overhead a silver jetliner slides eastward across cloudless skies ahead of the phlegmy growl of its passing. To the west, a curl of smoke from some valley mill further marks human intrusion.

But close overhead a familiar osprey, a twisting trout tightly clutched in its talons, rises and banks into the wind. I take Janet's hand in mine, squeezing it gently.

We are home. And intuitively I know, my search ended, I now must do my best to live a good life in a good place. Likely the last best place there is. My place.

Epilogue

IT IS DAWN of a gray, late-winter day on my place.

Below the shaded bluff with its clinging patches of soiled snow, the dark river flows briskly, audibly, beneath wisps of vapor hanging low over the riffles. Fragile ice crystals gird streamside boulders, and branches of a wind-felled spruce bob gently in the current eddying past the broken tree. The air is clean, sharp, as only the air of a Rocky Mountain morning can be. In the far distance I can hear the soulful cries of unseen geese.

I left the cedar house in the grayness of dawn, tracking across the hoarfrost carpet to where I now stand at the corner of the horse-pasture fence, surveying an awakening world. My pencil makes scratchy sounds on the lined paper of the cold tablet I cradle like some musical instrument I play silently, familiarly, despite cold-numbed hands and fingers.

To my right, a small band of shadow deer—half a dozen or more—cross the frozen ruts of my lane and walk into the dark pines beyond. They are too far away for me to hear the faint, furtive *tick* that their polished hooves make with each tentative step, but I know the sound and hear it in my mind. And I stand and watch their indistinct shapes ghost among the straight, gray-black tree trunks until there is nothing more to see.

Finally turning, I stare across the valley floor at the line of dark mountains beyond. Once, I know, another hunter stood on or near this very spot and stared at the same distant peaks. He felt the empty belly hunger only fresh meat can assuage; I feel a hollow soul hunger only the pursuit of wary wild things can relieve. Separated only by time, we remain blood brothers sharing a common place and need.

And as I walk his familiar paths, unseen to most modern men, I thank God for these majestic lands and the secretive wild creatures that inhabit them. For giving me a glimpse of such glories. For blessing me with a patience and understanding that builds perception, knowledge, and insight.

And I also thank my long-dead spirit brother for once passing this way. Without him and his requisite woodland skills, we could never fully understand — or truly appreciate — our own.